Touch and Go
The Nature of Intimacy
relating in the coming times

To Karen with
much love +
many Blessings!

Judy

Interact Publishing
P.O. Box 2185
Tijeras, NM 87059

First Edition

Made in Albuquerque, New Mexico USA

Cover Design: Maggie Macnab
Interior Design: Pamela Farrington
Editor: Karen Weaver
Proofreader: Eden Tatum Boric

Library of Congress Control Number: 2001099483

Borich, Judy G.
        Touch and Go the Nature of Intimacy
            1. Self-Growth
            2. Spiritual
            3. Relationship
            4. Psychology

ISBN 0-9641616-3-X

dedication and gratitude

This book is dedicated to my teachers. I thank my parents and my brother and sisters who had a hand in the shaping of my world. I honor the authors of the many books I have read and studied and the forces that came through their writings. I thank all those with whom I studied over my lifetime and especially the ones who had the courage to tell me when I was off track and who pointed the way back.

My clients have been teachers all along the way in my professional career and have been formative in the writing of this book. I thank them for their trust, for letting me so deeply into their lives and their hearts. I never, never, take this lightly.

I am thankful for the particular biology that lives in me. I thank my ancestors from whom I received the tendencies with which I was born. These tendencies have been great teachers. I am grateful for all the troubles in my life, for overcoming these has made me strong and sure.

For everyone who has ever loved me, I thank you. You live on in my heart even though you may have passed out of my life. You are not forgotten but remembered sweetly. For those who share the experience of connection and love with me now—my friends, my son and his family and especially my granddaughter, Maisie—you have taught me so much about the unconditional nature of true love.

To my lovely shining Gurumayi who showers me with blessings and bliss, I am forever grateful. To the One Omnipresent Heart who whole-heartedly holds us all, I thank you for imbuing us with love beyond imagination and belief. I am grateful for the perseverance of this great power that will plow through our defenses relentlessly so that we may live and feel this love.

Author's note to the reader:

*T*his is not a complicated book. The message is quite simple. I have repeated it in different ways again and again because there is a part of us that resists change or any new view.

This part of us is the ego. The ego's job is to keep us safe and maintain its own existence. Therefore, change is not popular with the ego. It will avoid all that threatens its dissolution. It is character- istic for the ego to think that it already knows everything, so why would it need to change? Intimacy is dangerous to the ego. The ego cannot tolerate the disintegration that begins with connection.

If you grasp the shift that is available here, you will be changed. So when you find that you are arguing and wishing for evidence and scientific logic, please know that you won't find much of it here. I have used just enough logic to try to interrupt the current view of the world enough for a new system of thinking to begin to form. For even though I am well grounded in science and understand the principles of quantum physics, mathematics, systems, theology, and biology, I leave the proof of theory to those who have done this already and are good at presenting information in a scientifically logical way.

The model you will find here is both intuitive and deductive. Spirit colors the deductions. The deductions here are informed by being open to the expansion and unfolding of alive and active mindfulness. The principles here are steeped in the subtle emotions and therefore are more reasonable than logical. Therefore, I have not included a bibliography but have replaced that aspect of book writing with a reading list. I am often asked for one, so here it is at the end of the book for those of you who are interested.

I don't pretend to think that reading about a model is the best way to absorb it—that may be an impossible task. The best way, of course, would be to experience the model. At my retreat center in New Mexico, people have an opportunity to come and experience what it is like to be related in such a setting, such an environment.

Those who have come there have urged me to write about the experience—to try to convey its magic, its safety, its expansive state. This is an attempt to answer their request.

I have been leading retreats for twelve years. They first began in Colorado with my colleague and friend, Barbara. They now take place on twenty acres southeast of Albuquerque, New Mexico. They are the joy of my life. With the wonderful surroundings, the openness of the people who come, their participation and trust, I never fail to be deeply moved. I learn with each new group.

I recommend that you read with your heart. The way to read is open, considering, curious, soft, and ready. Read with your awareness of the heart instead of just your intellect. It would be good if you could remember your heart-felt meetings, your heart-filled glimpses of what is being said here. That will help you to know how available intimacy is for everyone. My wish is that you will experience the essence of the model and that the message here will enhance your intimate life and open the way for more.

You will not find rules. This is not a self-help book. There will not be a thing for your intellect to do. You won't find a right way or a wrong one. You will simply be left with considering what works and doesn't work.

You will find the ideas in this book consistent with the twelve-step program that is a spiritual path itself. It is possible to walk into a room and pick out people who have done twelve-step work. These people know self-examination and self-reflection. The vibration of people in recovery is often well contained and respectful. The ego is operating in service of The Background.

I have a great deal of respect for those of you who have addressed addiction, for I think, in our society, we are mostly addicted. Our thinking is the thinking of addiction. Our thinking is that of attachment and of the unexamined life. I am very grateful to count myself as one of those recovering people.

Some of you will find yourself at a crossroads, a choice point, and an opportunity to take a new path. These junctures present themselves throughout our lives. It is often useful to have a map, pointing to another road, pointing the way to new territory. I am clear, however, that the journey is a personal one. Each person's path will have its own twists and turns, its own hardships and triumphs.

With our cultural isolation, our mobility, our absence of wisdom teachers, our cutting off from spirit and each other, we have less access to the maps of higher consciousness, the maps to expansion. We have lost our way.

Indicators of our lost nature are the signposts of social unrest and the contraction in our consciousness. This is evidenced in the rise of the use of depression and anxiety medications, the rise in crime rate, incarceration, increase in violence and terrorism, the disrespect for our environment and its resources, the high divorce rate, the suicide rate, alcoholism, homelessness, stress, anxiety, and despair.

Currently 53% of all marriages end in divorce. This doesn't count separations and dissatisfaction. If we had a way to measure that, what do you suppose we would find?

I am a teacher of sorts, a psychotherapist, a theologian, a philosopher, a lover of life. My life is embedded in a deep and lasting faith. In the heart, I know that all is well, that life is unfolding, that there is a Divine order. I am grateful for the intimate experiences in life, for they are the change makers, the catalysts, and the alchemy of evolution and transformation. Over the course of the years of living, I've been privileged and blessed, actually showered, with a magnitude of delicious intimacy.

I hear the cry, the calling of the people. I hear the yearning to have intimacy in their lives. I see people paying attention to the wrong thing, going after *things* instead of experience. They get into the presence of intimacy and do not know how to let the experience in. I see them living from their head, in the intellect, and out of touch with their hearts. This book is about the path back to the heart.

If you have connected with the background of life you may have your own name for it. People refer to the background of life in many ways:

> The Grand Design, Great Spirit, God, Lord,
> The Tao, Shiva, Allah, Jehovah, Atman,
> The Christ, Brahman, Mother-Father God,
> The Silence That Gives, One, Higher Consciousness,
> The Self, Yahweh, Higher Power.

This connection will be expanded as you learn to bring it into your relating, actually, when your relating moves inside of that connection.

If you are skeptical or closed to spiritual matters, that is fine, too. Much damage has been done by religion and in the name of God. People relating with the vastness of the background in which we are embedded have been squeezed into dogma and rules, thereby hurting them and cutting them off from Source. Past disappointments and hurts need to be addressed. It is fine and common to be mad about it. It is fine and common to have a contracted sense of Spirit.

Here and throughout the book, I am going to use more neutral words interchangeably to point to the vast background called spirit. I'll say Spirit, The Background, Our Creator, The Life Force and sometimes I will say God, The MYSTERY, The Divine.

You read whatever you read when you see these words and don't try to change your reactions. It is fine and common to have a reaction. Some people's access to The Background, to That Which Gives, is nature or a special, sacred relationship with a pet or a favorite grandmother. Whatever moves your heart, as you think of it, will work.

The model of *Touch and Go* sets us up in a system. The system has a structure that allows for growth and development. It allows for change, safety and communication that do not damage. There is room for autonomy and cooperation. All of this is held and fed by the background of Spirit.

The *Touch and Go* model is based on the principles of new science and the principles of ancient wisdom.

Throughout the book I use the pronoun *we*. This is because I am speaking in the language of inclusion. All of us are embedded in an unfolding culture and none of us is free from its influence. I am including myself as a student along the unfolding way and I'm very clear that we teach what we have to learn.

This book is not for everyone. It is for those of you who are tired of the old limited view of relating. I am not trying to prove anything or convince anyone. What I offer is up to you. It is for your consideration. Since I know that the map and the territory are not the same, I also know that the territory is vast. There is room for all points of view. I suspect there are as many means of reaching the vastness of the territory as there are people who search, but there is only one way. The way is through higher consciousness.

So let us get to the basics. Perhaps the path back is through the intellect and the scientific modality itself, this current paradigm in which we all are so enmeshed. It is, however, terribly slow. Perhaps it is best to allow for the alchemy of radically shifting living structures, the faster transformative action of a living system. Have we reached enough stress? Has the old way brought us enough pain? Have we "hit bottom?" Is it time yet?

Table of Contents

My propositions serve as

elucidation in the following way:

Anyone who understands me

eventually recognizes them as nonsensical.

When he has used them as steps to

climb up beyond them, he must, so to speak,

throw away the ladder after he has climbed up it.

He must surmount these propositions, then

he sees the world rightly. Whereof one cannot

speak thereof one must be silent."

- *Ludwig Wittgenstein*
from Tractatus Logic Philosophicus

Introduction

In each of us there is a seed. This seed contains the greatest power in the universe. This power, when unfolded, allows us to unite in consciousness with our Creator. Along with this seed comes the urge, the yearning for the fulfillment of our nature.

We are given glimpses throughout our lives of this ecstatic state. One of these times is when we fall in love. It is then that we enter the MYSTERY. We are lifted above the limits of the sense world and shown the expansive nature of consciousness itself. We are shown the glory of the heart.

As we answer this call to expand, we often get sidetracked or lost along the way. We may decide to pursue this glimpse. We try to get it back or have it longer. This uplifted state happens most often and profoundly in the experience of intimacy. We can get sidetracked there and much of the culture has indeed done that, been sidetracked into thinking relationships will provide the missing ecstasy.

We think that the experience occurs outside of ourselves and that another human is necessary, or even that a particular other human is necessary, in order to have the experience. This is a major mistake, for then we have to get the right conditions or the right person in order to get what we need. This always leaves us eventually disappointed, for no other human being is able to provide this uplifted state.

We may turn to fame or fortune or success or entertainment and become sidetracked there. When we get disappointed and discouraged, we may turn to the cheap transient thrills of alcohol, drugs, or sex to reach glimpses of this altered state. None of this fulfills ultimately and can even completely block the path.

The purpose of this book is to distinguish the true nature of intimacy and prepare us for its life-altering magic.

We do not generally have the training or practice of tuning ourselves in so that we are able to receive intimacy. It mostly happens as a surprise.

These glimpses are fleeting because we are not ready. Our nervous systems are weak; our minds flutter and are unable to focus. Our emotions overpower us and do not inform our intuition. We override our intuition in favor of something else.

Our bodies, our minds, our awareness, our intellect can be trained so that we are ready, so that we can register the vibrations of the mysterious.

The MYSTERY can only be pointed to. The sense of it can be grasped with our intuition and in our heart where the memories of such occasions are held for us. We know these important times by heart. The birth of a child, the tender memories of home, a great meal, a time in nature when we were moved to tears by the grandeur of it all—these are our reminders when we are stuck. The heart memories of these glimpses keep us cooperating with the unfolding until we are strong enough to live in that uplifted state, the state where we register fully the vibration of connection, connection with all, ONE.

This journey is for those who have joined the call to fully be in their own unfoldment. We will examine the kind of view of the world and thinking patterns of cause and effect that block MYSTERY's progress. We will look at how our view of people and relating is contracted and full of mischief. We will see what is needed to be ready, so that as the unfolding progresses, we can experience it.

We can learn to recognize the sidetracks and pull ourselves back from them. We can strengthen the nervous system and train the intellect to pull back from folly. We can learn stillness. We can practice being in the presence of another or others, allowing this place of mystery to show us the way.

We will find teachers and paths along the way. There are many teachers, we are all teachers, respectfully, even our enemies teach us well.

Teachers, if they are true, may only point the way. Each of us travels alone, even though we are entirely connected and loved and cherished. We have to come to terms with the paradox of both being alone and being connected and loved. Somehow, we are afraid of both. Perhaps the real job is to come to terms with fear itself.

I wish you well along the way. I wish many teachers and many teachings. May your journey bring you home in consciousness and may you accept where you are along the path and relish wherever it takes you as you unfold.

PART ONE

The Nature of Intimacy

The Promise of Intimacy

Intimacy is so elusive! We yearn for its experience and search for its evidence. We demand its presence and grieve its loss. As intimacy's delicious nature calls to us, we know intuitively that it is the vibration that fulfills life.

During these moments of intimacy, there is an energetic attraction and release. We are swept out of our ordinary selves into the heart of The Creator and everything gets changed.

We become unaware of time and our surroundings, unaware of our bodies and our personalities, our history or our future. We are lost in the moment where we feel connected.

There is an exhilarating feeling of being met, of being known, being able to communicate without words.

As the spark of intimacy leaps across the boundary between, it energizes us and brings us into the present, leaving us full and deeply alive.

Intimacy is a phenomenon, a happening, an occurrence, an experience that registers in the body in a particular way. The movement into intimacy leaves us shaken, moved emotionally, full of wonder, awe, and gratitude. It leaves us in an expanded state.

As our hearts become electrified by this phenomenon, consciousness expands, traveling out where we are able to behold that all is well.

This experience of intimacy makes no logical sense and cannot be held on to. The more we try to pursue it, the more elusive it becomes. The moment we notice, in our brain, that it is happening, it disappears.

Intimacy can happen to anyone and it doesn't even take a personal connection for intimacy to occur. In our culture we label this phenomenon falling in love or sexual attraction, however, the same experience can happen in a passing glance, without warning, with a complete stranger, and can be without any sexual or romantic content or charge.

We miss many moments of intimacy because we are so focused on romance. We are trained and tuned to notice it more when intimacy occurs with the opposite sex or with someone to whom we are attracted, who meets with our approval. Yet there are moments of intimacy with the earth, with a sunset, with the animals, with the moon and stars when we find ourselves in an expanded state.

The poets and mystics tell us this!

Although anyone can have the experience of intimacy, not everyone can move with it, be aware of it, and be ready for it again and again.

The vibration or frequency of intimacy is difficult to be with for very long. There is often a dissonance or discomfort at the edge of it, before the transformative moment, where the alchemy is ready to do its magic.

Right there, at the edge, when intimacy arrives, we have to be able to be still, staying there long enough to be found by the movement that wants to happen.

We have to be able to stay in the dissonance until being swept into our hearts, and into the heart of God.

This place of alchemy can cause great fear. It is a vulnerable place, a place where we fear we will lose ourselves.

And indeed we will! We will lose our own sense of our personalities and our bodies. As the ego dissolves all that remains is intimacy itself.

What if there is plenty of intimacy bringing us love, ecstasy, bliss, and connection, everywhere, all the time?

What if we are but blinded by our training and our expectations?

What if we are just not able to tolerate the experience because our nervous systems are too weak?

As our nervous system becomes strong and the mind able to concentrate, intimacy will occur in our consciousness more frequently and linger longer.

In a whole person, an actualized individual, a person centered in their heart, intimacy occurs quite often. That is why they are so content.

What if this vibration of intimacy is the entry, the window, into the Sacred Holiness of life? Suppose that we gift the world, each other, and ourselves by being able to receive this communion, this meeting from on high?

Wouldn't it be worth learning what it takes to be ready for it to register with us? Wouldn't it be worth it to be ready to join in consciousness, in the heart with the vibrational field of our Creator, connected with everything, integrated, whole with the universe, at last?

Through intimacy we are on a path beyond:

Beyond role

Beyond ideal

Beyond expectation and belief

Beyond the intellect

Beyond mind

Beyond materialism and knowledge

Beyond the senses

Beyond into Glory!

Go Beyond!

Working Definitions

In my study of dynamic, living relationships, what some of the participants would call closeness, I would call intimacy. Intimate relationships can be felt. It is in the atmosphere. It feels warm and open and inclusive. What others call intimacy, I would call *too* psychologically close. Those relationships feel exclusive and the participants seem distant and unreachable. It is isolating to be around them. It is obvious that we need to get clear on the terms.

INTIMACY — Touched together spiritually. The electrifying alchemy of life. The juice of life that we are yearning for.

TOUCH — The moments of intimacy.

GO — Distance, either psychological or physical.

CLOSE — Distinct from intimacy. The feelings we have after intimacy has passed.

TOO PSYCHOLOGICALLY CLOSE — When we hold a picture of the other person in our head based on history and relate from that picture as if we *know* them. It is also when you feel another's emotions and it is difficult to tell whose feelings are whose.

REFERENT — A composite "picture" or idea in our memory of how things *are* or *should* be.

AUTONOMY — Having a Self and a boundary separate from other people.

CENTER — The sense of your own presence, in your own energy field or container, apart from others. It is when you are distinct and not enmeshed with others.

CONTAINER — The energetic field around your body measurable through science. The place where you have room to be. Your own space.

RELATIONSHIP — The referent we have as individuals and a culture. There really is no such thing as a relationship. In truth what we refer to is a series of interactions over time, held in memory.

RELATING — The process of interacting.

BOUNDARY — A structure in consciousness that has an inside and an outside. It allows for energy to freely move in and out of the boundary. It selects certain energies to respond to and ignores other energy. It provides an internal environment.

INTERNAL STRUCTURES — These are the means of maintaining the internal environment or organization of a system. They are responsive to the energy that is running through the system and rejuvenate themselves. The environment maintains them and they maintain the environment.

HEALTHY SYSTEM — A dynamic, flexible, changing, self-regulating, self-growing environment that has a clear boundary separating it from the energies outside of itself. This boundary is open and lets in certain energies and disregards others. It is therefore self-selecting. Inside such a system, there is autonomy and cooperation.

TRANSFORMATION — A sudden radical alteration in con-scienceness.

Intimacy and Closeness

There is confusion about intimacy. There is confusion about closeness. I would call this confusion a collapse. A collapse happens when we are not clear about what we are talking about or what we believe.

When we say intimacy, we sometimes mean sex. Sometimes we mean we are familiar with someone, sometimes we mean we are close, and sometimes we mean we are attached.

Intimacy and closeness are not the same. One of the reasons we miss out on intimacy is because we have it so confused with feeling close. Intimacy is an experience and closeness is a feeling.

Intimacy and closeness cannot occur together, in the same moment. They are mutually exclusive and happen in sequence.

Intimacy occurs, then comes a time of closeness, then a movement to distance and then intimacy is able to happen again. It moves in a cycle of closeness, distance, intimacy, closeness and so on.

Infatuation, excitement, caring, dependency, understanding, desire, attraction, lust, and romance are also distinct from intimacy. As we know, much sex is far from intimate. In fact, we will often move too quickly into the sexual act in order to avoid intimacy and then say that we were intimate.

Let us take intimacy out of the confusion. Intimacy has its own flavor. It is distinct. There is no mistaking its vibration.

Closeness, however, has an entire range of feeling.

At one end of the closeness range, there is a sweet completion and rest after moments of connection, a certain enjoyment and musing about what has just happened. There is a languishing in the ripples of the intimate vibration.

This kind of closeness is nice and to be savored, for sure. It is the natural fallout of intimacy. But when we stay there too long or try to make this the goal, closeness begins to turn to mischief.

At the other end of the range of closeness, we find major trouble. It can get quite constrictive. Too much closeness can get over-connected and possessive. The head takes over and we think we own the other person.

This psychological closeness is full of our assumptions about the other. We think we know them, when we merely know about them. This kind of closeness can feel like being smothered. We feel that we will be swallowed up and have no room to be. We resent and become defensive about the assumptions the other has made about us. We argue about clarifying those assumptions. At this stage, there is a lot of struggle or fighting to pull apart and have our own space again.

Liking for, affinity, and fond remembering are all a part of the time after intimacy. They are the time of closeness.

When we fail to notice the difference between intimacy and closeness, we can fall into a familiar trap. We cling to the comfort of closeness and ensure that intimacy cannot occur again.

We all love the precious intimacy and closeness that begins much relating, but quite quickly, we take the precious moments and wrap them in pursuit, thinking, and ideals.

This closeness, this over-connectedness with and possessiveness of the other takes place in our heads. It can become an obsessive demand for a remembered experience.

When closeness is most negative, it is imposed, intrusive, and jealous. It is the playing out of insecurity, excessive identification with another, separation anxiety, and fear of being left alone. In conflicted closeness, we cannot stop thinking about the other. This can be pining after them or it could be hatred of them. Ultimate negative closeness is when the wished-for other is a phantom in the brain and there is no actual exchange. This can turn into stalking.

As we have too much attention on the other, we become off balance with ourselves and therefore, unavailable for intimacy.

We go after the experience and we go after people in a desperate attempt to get more, to make a relationship out of it. This pursuit pulls us off balance, makes us act with the craziness of being in love. We can become pathetic, distracted, and without the moderation of reason. Without the wisdom of the heart, the head takes us on a roller coaster ride.

We get tired of closeness. We need time on our own. We need a break from so much overlapping. We need to have a break from closeness to regain a sense of being an individual, to have some autonomy, free of the collapsed energy.

The False Self

The false self consists of a collection of compensatory behaviors that we have developed to try to make in it life. Compensatory behaviors are our emotional programs for happiness based on the imprinting of early childhood. They are based upon a child's logic and they may still be hidden in the unconscious. They include attachments, aversions, expectations, and demands. It is what we do to manage the impression others have of us. We may please others or lie or put on airs. We may do too much or try to fix up our looks. We may collect material things to enhance ourselves, or become famous or funny. The false self is emotionally dishonest and inauthentic. It is a lie, but many of us have been presenting this false self for so long we think it is true.

The false self is like those life-sized cardboard figures of the stars at the movie theatre. We are holding out the false self, like the cardboard figure, in front of us. Lights are shining on it and we hope that other people think it is real. The trouble is, if you peek around at the back of the figure, you see a shadow. Since we are holding the figure out in front, we are looking at the back side. We are looking at the shadow. We try to hide our dark nature or our shadow self from others. If you hang around someone long enough, you will begin to see their shadow and yours cannot stay hidden.

An unexamined shadow follows the false self around and peeks out from time to time. An unexamined and untamed shadow is a dangerous thing. Many people have jumped into relating with others without first learning about their shadow and have been hurt. We must face our shadow nature or it takes over our life.

You cannot know a person by what they say. In the beginning of meeting, we are managing the impression others have of us. If you do not allow for this, you may fall for charm and get tricked. The way you get to know someone is to hang out with them over time and see who they are by how they are being, not by what they say about themselves. We hardly ever want to take the time for this.

We have to make sure that our vibration matches our mouth, that their vibration matches their mouth.

When we think the job is to get to know the other person, we are into the third bit of mischief. We conveniently forget that they are doing impression management with us. We collect a composite picture of the other based on what they say and do and what others say about them plus the collected memories of our time spent with them. We are now forming the referent to which we will compare further interactions.

We talk about their personality and their body and their thoughts and emotions and our history with them as if that was all there is. We are not paying attention to the background, the unsaid, the soul, the heart of the other.

Then there is further trouble: we have a shared cultural view of relating, strongly believed and wished for, largely unexamined. This is the cultural referent. We talk about our dreams of a relationship with the other to see if we would be compatible and if we agree on the same *picture* of relating.

We have expressions such as my *better half*. We believe that alone, we are less than whole, incomplete, one half. We believe that one half and one half equal a whole. While this may be true in mathematics, it becomes trouble in relating. We turn to our partners to bolster ourselves, to be validated and soothed, and we become disillusioned when they are not able or willing to provide what we want. We feel neglected and take it personally.

If I am not whole, and I expect you or the relationship to complete me, I am in trouble. If I think you are not whole and need something from me, I am in danger of becoming depleted. We are in a tug of war to get the seemingly scarce amount of nurturing. In this power struggle, the energy of each person is either being sapped or controlled.

Each fights for control of the situation by demanding more from the other or avoiding the demands of the other.

By now, the phenomenon of intimacy has subsided or stopped and each person is taking their disappointment out on the other.

Each is becoming demanding, outraged, and panicky; feeling rejected; and complaining that the other isn't giving them what they need, what was implicitly promised at the beginning. This is a huge burden and a mistaken concept to think that the other human is the source of the initial experience.

Each individual is out of touch with the expanded states of life, out of touch with the expansive nature of consciousness itself. Each person is left with trying to get what they intuitively know is possible from the contracted forms of life. Symbiosis and fusion or cutting-off and isolation become the only options. Both people become off balance and both are missing that which allowed it all to work in the first place—the expansive state, the place of the heart.

Eventually we deplete ourselves, we have nothing left of ourselves. After being shown a glimpse of the expanded state in the moments of intimacy, we do not know how to move back to center. Everything gets collapsed into fusion or enmeshment into the state of mental anxiety and fear.

Enmeshment is painful. It is painful to be a part of this activity, to be caught up in the cultural view of relating and stuck there.

Closeness does not create intimacy—it is the fruit of intimacy.

Clinging to togetherness and the idea of closeness will ensure that intimacy cannot occur again. Touch and clutch, chase and retreat, the struggle for distance and closeness can consume the entirety of relating.

If one or both gives in and submits to the control of the other a sort of uneasy peace remains. This can continue as long as each person stays in their role, which is a contracted state. Hidden or expressed resentment and undermining usually accompanies this arrangement. We are role-playing with an idea of how it could be. Underneath the relating, disappointment prevails or is repressed into denial.

Without some intervention, we are destined to play out the models we grew up with. We are destined to only live inside our protective compensatory behaviors. Without an internal shift, there is no other alternative. We are role-playing with no internal resources. We are caught in stylized, superficial ways of relating. Out of touch with our subtle energies. Out of touch with our emotional wisdom. Out of touch with the heart. Out of touch with the present. Out of touch with awareness. We are lost in the limited moves the intellect can figure out. We act like we are being intimate without being stirred, without transformation. Our intimacy is thought up and then acted out. We are wounded and we are wounding others.

It is not enough to simply get another idea of how it should or could be. We have to do the difficult internal work of altering ourselves.

When the old way gets too restrictive, too contracted, it is no wonder we fight. We fight to try to pull apart. We try to pull apart from the referent we see that the other is holding of us and the roles we are playing because we intuitively know we are more than that. We try to pull out of the categories and roles, pull out of too much closeness, physical or mental. We try to be free of the collapsed energy and regain our sense of expansion.

We are left feeling empty and hollow and not knowing how to have what we are missing, what we so desperately yearn for. We are left in despair and depression and discouragement. We are angry. At this point, we need to set aside our false pride to ask for help.

We have to become ready and willing to see where we are tied and contracted, where we are stuck. Then, we get to work and we ask to be willing to surrender all of our firmly held beliefs. Without the recognition and movement into the expansive states of being we can only be an image, play a role.

Romance is a poor attempt to hide the true self and gain acceptance. We have to admit that we have left our heart.

The Current Model for Relating

Beginnings are bright poignant encounters that imitate the movies and romance novels. We are swept up and away into intimacy's magic! We know that we have found *the one*. We can speak about anything, spend long hours in the company of each other, and so on. After a time—and how quickly it can happen!—disappointment sets in as the power struggles begin.

THIS IS HOW IT WORKS:

Following the moment or moments of intimacy, there is a quick assessment of the possibility of relationship. For instance, we like this, we do not like that, they remind us of someone, we size up their appearance, and so on. We consult our brains to see if this could be a possible relationship or fling, a friendship, or whether we should disregard them.

We are so starved to be connected and think it can only happen if there is romance involved. We shut down to others who don't qualify fairly soon because we are in pursuit of romance. After a very short time—interviewers say only a few seconds—we already have a *take* on the other person and they have been defined and classified.

If our interest is captured because they fit into the right category, we turn our attention to keeping this phenomenon of connection around, box up the whole experience and call it *a relationship*. The mischief has begun!

Each person makes the mistake of thinking this wonderful, energetic meeting is coming from the other person, from their actions or from inside of them.

We imagine the other, rather than Spirit, to be the source of the intimacy. We begin the pursuit for the reoccurrence of the uplifting phenomenon, calling it falling in love.

As the mischief continues, we go into a mode of impression management, making ourselves attractive to the other. We carefully play out what we think they want of us. Our attention is on the other, to keeping them around, pleasing them, so they will stay and the wished-for experience can be repeated.

Second-Hand Relating

Without knowing the difference between *knowing about* and *experiencing directly*, we end up with second-hand relating.

In second-hand relating, we are tied to the past and keep referring to the memory of the past as if it was what actually happened and not our interpretation. We act is if what we think happened in the past will be what is happening in the future. *Knowing about* is stored, collected into the memory, and referred to. We collect data about someone, gathering evidence to substantiate our already-established idea of how they are. We base this upon time spent together, things they have shared, experiences we have had, things others say about them, our projections and desires.

After a while, we think we are able to guess what the other wants or what their reactions will be in a given situation. We will base our behavior on their imagined reaction. For instance, we may withhold a communication because we are sure they will be upset by it. We fear their upset and therefore justify the withholding.

This way of relating through a referent or imagined picture of the other leaves us relating in stylized, automatic, and predictable ways. We eventually cannot tell what are their feelings and what are our own.

There is more than one kind of referent. There is the kind that is formed spending time with another, a collection of our impressions of them and our judgments, opinions, and comparisons. The other kind is a referent about relating in general. This would include our strongly held idea of what we want in a relationship and the cultural referent about how the world and relating *should be*.

Let us consider our ideas about relating and how it *should be* and see if they, too, lead us to second-hand relating.

First, let us consider our personal view of relating, our desires and wishes and longings. As a child, we need to receive enough nurturing and we need adult caretakers who are dependable and emotionally available. They need to be able to be there for us, connecting with us and giving us affection. Too many of us did not receive this nurturing or enough of it for various reasons. Perhaps the parent was too young or depressed, or addicted. Perhaps there was a war or poverty or too many other children. Maybe there was illness or tragedy. Maybe there was violence or simply poor parenting.

What a child does then is look around for something better to dream about. They begin to assemble a composite picture of what they would prefer. They pick a mommy from a television show, a daddy from visiting their friend's house, an income level that would fulfill their desires.

Many decisions are made during childhood such as:

I'll never be like that when I grow up.
I'll never let someone tell me what to do.
I'll never be this vulnerable again.
I'll show them.
I must be bad.
If I were only better, my mommy or daddy wouldn't hurt me.

These decisions about life and other people and ourselves influence our whole lives until they are examined and healed. These decisions could be determining our relationships.

Since trouble does happen to many of us and perhaps we didn't get enough nurturing, we weren't cared for thoroughly or we couldn't really depend on anyone, we go out to fulfill the void, this needy hole. We look for someone to take care of us! We look for someone or something to fulfill our needs, to love us, to fix us, to complete us, to pay enough attention.

Almost always, we are disappointed. Disappointment gathers and accumulates and we conclude that there must be something wrong with us.

Then we have the cultural referents, an *ideal* way of how relating should be. We end up relating through a referent of how it is supposed to be, based on novels and movies and media. We compare what is happening in the moment to the ideal, the pictured expectation. This never allows for being in present time with another. The culturally held ideas are based on rapture and romance. The head is very sure it knows what romance is and the heart gets left out.

These cultural referents turn into myths. The fairytales and fantasies turn into entitlements or certain inalienable rights.

Our stance in the world and with each other becomes demanding. We feel entitled to a relationship. What we mean is, we feel entitled to this picture of what is in our head. We are certain that it will feel a certain way when we *get it right*.

WE DEMAND:

☑ To be happy ever after

☑ To not have to be alone

☑ To have company

☑ To grow old with someone

☑ To feel safe, secure, have life be easier

☑ To have our needs fulfilled

☑ To be taken care of

☑ To have sex

☑ To have great sex

☑ To have enough affection

☑ To be understood and listened to

☑ To have children

☑ To be with our children

☑ To get what we want

☑ To have common interests

☑ To not have trouble

☑ To be in control of what happens in our lives

☑ To have our needs met

When we don't get what we are expecting or when something thwarts or takes away one of these demands, it leads to complaining. Complaining always contaminates an environment for relating.

We blame the other for not providing what was present in the beginning, for not fulfilling our needs, for not spending time with us, for not nurturing us, for not giving us what we want, for not making us happy. What a burden to put on another human being! What a burden to put on relating!

We act as if our complaining will change things, that complaining will get the other to change. In fact, the complaining will ensure that the other will not change or give us what we demand!

As we try to change the other or mold ourselves to them, we become involved with gathering advice, gossiping about them to others and gathering agreement, getting very solid about how they are, of how we are, and how the relationship is.

In other words, we are conducting our relationships like petulant children.

We may become controlling, using manipulation and games to try to get our way. Relating is not an agreement to run each other's lives, to make another like you or to fit them into our expectations of how they should be or what should be happening. We cannot own another human.

We think that what we think is right and we do not discern the truth from the trash in our minds.

The result of all this leaves us tied to our ideas and expectations, tied to our feelings and emotions, with no other basis for relating, no presence, no other really, except the one in our rigid, made-up minds.

We don't even see the other after a while. Thinking you *know* someone falls far short of what is possible with him or her. It is limiting to you and to them. Familiarity can get in the way of intimacy. We really cannot directly know each other in the intellect.

All we can know is to know about one another's patterns and tendencies.

When closeness remains for too long or is grasped for or becomes the goal itself, it can become this obsessive demand for an idealized experience.

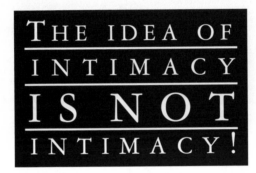

THE IDEA OF
INTIMACY
IS NOT
INTIMACY!

"*Romantic love is a grave social disease.*"

-Plato

Referent and Reification

The brain is efficient. It is splendid at classification and comparison. In an instant, it picks up an impression, evaluates a situation, and compares it with past experience. The brain instantly knows something about what is happening. This is a great survival technique. It quickly sorts out the enemy and helps keep us safe.

How quickly this process happens! It happens without our effort. We walk into a room full of people and click, click, click—the brain begins its sorting. People get sorted into yes, no, maybe. We know who is a possible romance or friend, whom we want to interact with, who is neutral, and whom we wish to avoid.

We have a pattern or array of patterns and preferences already established in the psyche. We come with some of these tendencies and are imprinted or impressed with others. These patterns are especially impressed into the psyche in the formative years but they also accumulate all through our lives.

It is as if we are an antenna selecting the vibrations that match our patterns out of all possible vibrations. We notice only what we are programmed to notice. The Hindus call these tendencies *samskaras*.

We know that whatever room we are sitting in now, as we read this, is full of wave patterns or vibrations. All of these vibrations are not registering with us. Television waves, radio waves, sounds and light waves outside of our range, we aren't picking up. Our receiver just disregards what it is not designed for.

This is the way it works with people. Have you noticed that when you are attracted to someone, their irritating traits seem to be invisible? It is only after a few months that we begin to notice the negative things. We simply did not pick them up before. We notice what we notice very selectively.

You meet someone and decide they are a yes, so you decide to spend some time together. While you are sitting with them, your brain begins its sorting. You have conversation, getting to know each other. However, there are really two conversations going on. There is the talking and there is the silent conversation, taking place in each other's

23

brain about the other. These are usually judgments such as "I like this," I don't like that," "that reminds me of," and so on.

If this meeting went well and everything adds up to wanting to meet again, then again you meet. Both conversations continue, gathering more impressions. There is a point when the impression becomes reified or solid and we now know the other person. If they show up a third time and are different than the first two times, we say something like, "What is wrong?" or "You aren't yourself today!" We act as if we know who they are already. We act as if it is possible ever to know them.

This is because we have already formed a referent or picture, a mental representation in our brain about how they are. This process kills many relationships. It happens quite fast and we cannot stop it. Studies of interviewers tell us it only takes a matter of seconds to make up our minds of how people are. We all know this—in fact, we try to make a good first impression.

When this process of referencing is the only mechanism we use for relating, it leads to too much psychological closeness. It can play out in a great deal of mischief.

We can operate automatically from our referents or we can study the referents and know when they are operating and be with something bigger. We can be with the person directly. We can get to know them or experience them directly. Knowing about someone is very different than being with them in experience.

Direct knowing is what happens in the vibration of intimacy. It has no words and cannot be referred to through words. It is happening and then it is gone. The other person's essence registers in the heart. It can only be remembered as a sensation in the heart.

Thinking: The Block to Intimacy

There is a fundamental flaw in the way we view relating. The flaw lies in our view of the world, in our limited thinking about how life works. This system of thinking is ruining our relationships.

Our system of thought is based on our world-view and so is our language. A world-view is a way to organize the world. It is not necessarily the truth about the direct and true nature of reality. Therefore, any world-view distorts. It distorts simply because it is a representation of an agreed upon view or structure.

When we travel or live in a culture that is very different than our own, we find out that our world-view is not the way the world is for everyone. It can be very upsetting and disorienting. We call it culture shock!

For the last few hundred years, we have viewed the world and each other through a system of thought called scientific thinking or Newtonian/Cartesian thought. This view gives us an ordered and seemingly secure and knowable world. It protects us from the chaos behind the system. The important features of our view are:

The world is out there, fixed and knowable.

What is real can be measured and observed.

Our five senses give us accurate knowledge of the world.

The world that is out there and measurable can be categorized.

The nature of the world is dualistic— good/bad, right/wrong.

There is a hierarchy—some things and some people are more important than others.

The operating principle of the system is comparison. Comparing is the action in this system, so things can be sorted into categories.

The prize is knowledge. You have to have knowledge about the world in this system, so you know how to get money that will get you more prizes such as material things and influence over others. Then you can rise higher in the hierarchy.

The intellect is best equipped to deal with this kind of world-view, so we have focused much on the intellect, depending on it to tell us about the world.

This is not true in every culture. For instance, in Bali the heart and the Gods are the center of the world-view. In Bali, it is the relating that holds importance rather than knowledge.

Our mind is able to hold a picture, an idea, and so it does. The comparing mechanism is quite fast and moments of experience are compared with an array of experiences in the past and sorted into good/bad/better/best and so on.

Our brain stays very busy, spending lots of time collecting ideas and information and manipulating and sorting and acting from the conclusions. We stay inside the limited nature of our intellect trying to get ahead in the world. Life lived inside the intellect is reduced from a dynamic, ever-changing phenomenon into an object. This gives us a sort of shorthand way to explain, predict, know, and understand—really, a way to control the world.

We can notice certain things and ignore other things and we do. We are quite selective in where we put our attention.

We take an abstract phenomenon and define it in language, describe it, compare it, and based on this sorting process, we box it up and make it into a thing. This thing can now be referred to. This is done very efficiently with the intellect, without our effort. It is automatic. This process is the process of reification.

In this way, the mind keeps things in a fixed state. It makes every phenomenon into a thing and therefore static, not dynamic, dead.

We become trapped in this system of thought and thinking and view it as though it were truth. We view our perceptions as truth, even though we logically know they deceive, distort, and are limited. We view logic as truth and we view the results of scientific method as truth.

We worship science. It has become everything. God becomes anthropomorphized—an aged man in the sky who has a white beard and lots of fury and power. Spirituality becomes religion—full of rules and dogma. Love becomes a feeling in the body and a set of actions, so we can know and measure if it is happening. We say things like "If you loved me you would ..."

In this way, in the brain's process of reifying the human being, a person becomes a body with a mind and personality, a role, a possession, able to be categorized and nothing more.

People become things to manipulate and know. Relating becomes relationship, a noun, a thing to be worked on and talked about as if it could be found somewhere.

In close examination, there is no such thing as a relationship. What we call a relationship is merely a series of conversations and interactions over time, held in memory. Memory is fallible, inaccurate, and selective. We do not act as if this were true.

We disregard that which cannot be perceived with the senses or proven by scientific method. Knowing, the prize of this system, blocks direct experience, blocks the sensation of the heart of intimacy.

We relegate intuition, wonder, inspiration, awe, direct knowing, and agape as the stuff of the unknowable world and believe it is inaccessible to us. It is true, these phenomena are directly inaccessible in a limited view. These phenomena have no register in the intellect. If we believe that intellect is all there is, we miss a great deal.

There are only so many movements you can make inside the intellect. The result is recycling of thoughts and therefore, repetitive behavior cycles. We become entangled in the web of the intellect, lost from the experience of creation.

There is not enough room in our system of thought, in our language, in our intellect, for honoring the higher states of being. There is only room in expanded consciousness.

The scientific method, by itself, provides no values. Yet it has crept into every aspect of our lives rather than staying within its limitations.

Our view of the world has become outdated. Based on the findings of quantum physics, based on the scientific system itself, it is outdated and disproved. Quantum physics tells us there is no world out there, fixed and knowable.

The new sciences, such as quantum physics and the study of systems, tell us that human consciousness participates in the edition of the reality that meets our eye at any given moment.

There is no objective reality. The observer, the experimenter always affects the experiment. We live in a world of flux—a world that is more characterized by vibration than anything solid at all.

Human consciousness has not shifted to include the findings of quantum physics, of systems theory. This is reflected in how we relate. We are blocked by our world-view, which is fixed by our language. Remember the ego's job is to resist change.

We have not examined how a non-fixed, vibrating world could affect our view of relating, our experience of ourselves and life itself. We are living cut off from that which could fulfill life, that which is behind our system of thought, that which isn't sensed by the five senses.

We are trained to disregard the heart, the place of intuition, of MYSTERY and spirit. All that is immeasurable and in the background awaits our attention.

The way out of this mess is not to give up the intellect, relegate it to the category of the not useful, or try to overcome it. When we attempt to get out of the trap of our addiction to answers and things, we become more trapped, for we are trying to use the faculties of the system to get out of itself. This is not possible. We become dualistic and view the old system as wrong and some other way as right.

This is the folly of the new age thinking. When you make one system wrong in favor of a new system, you are still trapped in the first system because you are in duality. The more you try to get out of a system, the more you are in it. That which you resist, persists. It is like those bamboo woven puzzles where you stick your finger in each end. The more you pull on your fingers, trying to remove them, the more stuck they get. The way out of the puzzle is to relax the fingers. The way out of our old thinking is to let it be and relax, letting the background become the foreground.

The way out is through expansion, expansion beyond the intellect into the realm of awareness that is far more vast and fast than the intellect. We need to respect and honor the intellect and let it be useful for what it does well.

Something gets stopped by the material world. For our relationships, to fulfill our lives, we must expand beyond the intellect. Being stuck with only the intellect will limit our unfolding, our developmental process.

There in the expanded state, we will discover that all of creation is far bigger than our intellect. It is a place that cannot ever be proven by us, but is noticeably subjective. We will find that meaning is not in things, it lies inside of us and between us, behind us in the background. We are imbued with the vibration of Spirit, carrying with it energy and information for our fulfillment. We will view people or objects as they really are, dynamic and ever-changing, full of surprise and delight.

The soul loves expansion, yearns for it, and craves its fruits. One of the fruits of expansion is intimacy.

As we look upon an object as a thing, it becomes desecrated. When we look upon a subject and see the nothingness, the silence, the vastness which gives, the divinity that permeates it, it becomes a sacred dynamic phenomenon, bringing forth the blessing and the life force locked into it.

How can this happen? How can we expand in conscious awareness to include more than the limiting intellect?

We can consider and understand contraction and expansion. We can look at our own contracted state that is causing the trouble in our relating. We can ask. We can ask to be expanded into the consciousness where we can experience intimacy.

The alternative is too small, too contracted, and too full of suffering and pain. Staying closed and limited in our view and having this reflected in our relating keeps us addicted to quick fixes, to answers and techniques.

We can stay stuck in old patterns of behavior. We can remain in the mundane world of the brain where we are left with flat rules for behaving, left with social structure. We can be focused on what we can get, what we can accumulate. We can accumulate things and people and experience. We can have the products and skip the path.

What we get from things contracts us, limits us, uses our energy on that which goes away. This will leave us burned out and despairing. We will be left with nothing but memory and you know how predictable that is!

Relating based on thinking, based on how to, based on technique, can keep us stuck in old patterns of behavior or it can prompt us to move through them. First, we may have to get disgusted enough to find a different way. All trouble has the possibility of teaching us. Perhaps we have to stay in the mundane brain world and suffer enough in order to wake up to another possibility.

We can keep the view we have, study it, know how it works through us, find out its limitations and ask to be moved beyond.

We can learn to overcome our training and our tendencies in our relationships. We do this first by noticing that the way we conduct our relationships is not in accordance with reality.

We can let the intellect do its job, negotiating its part of life. Consciousness can expand us so that we may register the states beyond the senses, so that we are able to register the states beyond the intellect. The states of intimacy include the heart-filled states of intuition, illumination, direct knowledge, enlightenment, and union.

*e*

have become

objects to ourselves.

We have to go forward beyond reason

to discover mind and nature

are both simply different movements

of one absolute Spirit.

Spirit is not one apart from many,

but the very process

of the One expressing itself

through the many."

-Schelling

A Shift in View

Much more is possible than operating in the world with only a brain and five senses, thinking we are inside a body peeping out onto a fixed world. Scientific reality works on the phenomena of mass, energy, information, change, space, and time, but has limits when viewing the vast nature of the mystery beyond the sensory world.

The current scientific view of the world has gone unchallenged for nearly 300 years. This view has lasted so long because it so closely matches what our perceptions tell us.

The last major upheaval in a world-view came in the 1600s with the findings of Copernicus. He found that we were not the center of the universe and that the sun does not move around the earth. The egocentric view of mankind shifted. Copernicus could not publish his findings while he was alive because the entrenched view of the times was so directly opposed to his findings and people would have had to change too drastically. It was many years after his death that his findings were confirmed through replication and a shift in world-view began to happen.

To demonstrate how slowly our world-view changes, we have only to look at our language. We say, the sun comes up and goes down. These phrases match our perception, but not the truth of what is actually happening.

Even though we know the true behavior of the sun, our behavior related to the sun has not changed! Remember, it has been over 300 years since Copernicus!

Our present system was completely brought into question by science itself with the emergence of quantum physics in the early 1900s. Yet our thinking and our world-view, along with our institutions and strongly held beliefs about how the world works, is only now breaking down. The old view is being challenged.

With the work of Werner Heisenberg, we move into the uncertainty principle and shift from parts to the whole. Albert Einstein teaches us relativity and that energy and matter are interchangeable. David Bohm shows us the unfolding nature of the implicate order into the explicate order. Max Planck, who discovered quantum energy packets, indicates the alive nature of space. Humberto Maturana and Fransisco Varela have worked in the biological field as neuroscientists and have findings that they call structural determinism, that show that there is no fixed world out there that we can *know*. Their findings indicate that our world is based on our internal structure and arises with our interaction with the world. Therefore, we bring forth a world, rather than observing the world. We each live in our own world.

Ilya Prigogine, in studying systems, describes alive, dynamic systems far from equilibrium that are self-organizing and self-generating. He talks of dissipative structures that are not linear and that, at the point of stress, or what he calls bifurcation points, transform and reorganize the system, allowing for its growth and development, its evolution. These and other leading edge thinkers bring with them a new emerging view. They bring the view of the interactive nature of reality.

With the advent of heart transplant research and the study of the recipient and the donor, evidence is being gathered that the body is not just a mechanistic device with the brain running everything and the heart just a pump. Peptide receptors are found all over the body and the reports from heart transplant recipients indicate that the heart has memory. The heart remembers! The whole nervous system is brain-like.

To summarize: These findings indicate that everything is mostly space and flux. All is vibrating and connected and everything is affected by and affecting everything else all the time.

Things arise out of the interaction between the observer and the whole quantum soup of creation, so the observer is as important and active in the unfolding as that which is viewed. In fact there is no that which is viewed in any fixed and knowable way.

The world, its meaning, arises in the moment of viewing and is unique to each of us.

This new information from science has the potential to shift the foundation of what we are. This information will shift the world-view of anyone who considers deeply. What constitutes the world and our participation in our reality changes dramatically!

When matter breaks down into molecules and further into electrons, protons, and neutrons, it is still matter, a thing that can be measured according to Newtonian/Cartesian scientific principles.

When those particles are examined more closely by more sophisticated means, they become smaller and smaller entities. A quark is not a particle. It is a wave-like, particle-like, vibration that is constantly changing.

The world is vibrating. The particle nature breaks down at the point of quanta and what is left is a phenomenon. Quarks are vibrational phenomena of wave patterns which are not constant. These waves, this motion, indicate interactions rather than things.

If we took one molecule and blew it up into gigantic proportions, it would look like the night sky. We would see lots of space and some twinkling. There is only vibration, activity.

It is like this: we are designed to see certain vibrations and not others, according to our limited physiology, our culture, our training, our tendencies, our history, our programming.

There is no objective reality. This does not mean that there is nothing out there. It just means that whatever is out there cannot be directly experienced. It is only experienced by the limitations and design of our apparatus. There are only a whole lot of possibilities that do have limits, but those limits are beyond our senses. We draw in our version of the world by our attention, our tendencies, habits and beliefs, our thoughts and actions, our vibration, our heart.

The bad news is that our attention, our tendencies, habits and beliefs, our very thoughts and action, our vibration, our hearts are vibrating and changing and very little of it is in our control. It is all just happening. It is happening according to our design, our vibration, and our intellect is insufficient to will it to be different than it is.

To draw out a different world would take a shift in consciousness. To change the world, the observers must change. We do not exist as *things* and do not generate a different view. As our conscience expands, so does our view of the world.

Much mischief has been made by *New Age thinking* about how much power we have to create. Using the intellect, in a contracted state, we have no power to change any of it. In an expanded state, we are all powerful. Creation is ongoing and happening and we are joined with it. To speak about creating as an action is uninformed. It is also disappointing when we are told we can create and then bad things happen. We can then only be left with self-blame and no power.

Since everything is in flux and constantly changing, we are vibrating and are being bombarded by vibrations that are constantly changing and uplifting us. We are given the joy of awareness, the ability to be able to notice the unfolding and participate in it fully. As we feel it, rejoice with it, go with it, our hearts leap with wonder at it all. What a ride! As bad things happen, we experience that, too. We stay in the observer state, in equipoise.

When we are vibrating at a higher frequency, when we are expanded in consciousness, the whole world appears differently.

Without the participation of our particular vibration patterns, there is no differentiation, there is only undifferentiated vibration.

We form our world out of this raw material of vibration through our apparatus. We draw out of the whole only what we are programmed to see. We are programmed to see what our past and our tendencies are programmed to see.

This is sort of like Midas touching gold. Everything is vibrating and then we, a vibration, lock in with another vibration and it appears solid.

We are participators in the hologram. We are vibrating, unfixed entities, interacting with the vibrating, constantly changing phenomena of the universe.

There is good news! Our equipment is expandable. In its expanded state, it can pick up more vibration. This happens in awareness. It occurs in the heart, in the body, in the mind, everywhere all at once.

This expansion is the key to life. It is expanded consciousness. There is extraordinary wisdom in expanded consciousness. It is shown to us through eastern philosophy, in the lives and writings of the mystics of all religions, including Mystical Christianity. Some can point to the deep maps of consciousness embedded in the Bible, in the Kabbalah, in the Yoga Sutras in the Upanishads, and in the Tao of life itself.

Will we go *out there* in a fixed world that we learn to manipulate to our own benefit, or will we join in the hologram and participate in the movements of the whole—both affecting life and being affected by life in a dynamic, ever-expanding way? Will we move from the sure and predictable to the uncertain and emerging world?

A Vibrating World

We are imbedded in a holomovement, the movement of everything. The movement itself moves us. Places, people, things move to and away from us and blow about like clouds materializing and diminishing in the sky. They come close, sometimes there is a spark and then they move apart and disintegrate. It is the design of life.

We can join the design and move with the movement of life, enjoying what comes our way and watching what departs, or we can suffer and resist and think that it should be different.

The rest of this book is about removing those obstacles that prevent you from wholeheartedly joining the dance. It is about studying what makes us suffer and allowing for the expansion into what is real.

There is a part of us, found in the inner stillness, that is connected with this grand design. There is a part that intuitively knows when to join the coming together and when to watch the breaking apart. This part of us is unharmed by the circumstances of life. It is our cultural training that interrupts our experience of the whole. It is our world-view that breaks the whole into parts, leaving us discon-nected. When the surface of our awareness connects with our deeper nature, we connect with the rhythms of life.

When we have not distinguished, through study and self-examination, our cultural view, our tendencies and habits, we remain embedded in them. We sink into the bog of the world and we suffocate and wilt.

There are times when life offers each of us a window into the eternal, a chance to join in the deeper nature of life. In western culture, we are losing this. We are sinking into the bog of stress, burnout, dis-couragement, depression, and despair.

We need a new model of relating that corresponds and fits with the world as it occurs. Viewing our world, especially people and ourselves, as vibration, could have huge impact on our experience of being related.

People are no longer things but vibrational phenomena vibrating with other vibrating bodies, all connected by the vibrations between them. There is no empty space. Empty space is alive with the movement of vibration connecting us all. We can no longer be observers on the sidelines. All is connected, interconnected, sharing and exchanging vibration, never the same, always changing.

Relationships are no longer a thing to be referred to in the ideas of our brain. Relating comes alive, is a vibrant, ever-changing phenomenon worthy of our curiosity, located everywhere, registering in the heart.

We are aware of how environmentally sensitive we are, knowing that vibrations in everything are affecting us always. We are living as if we were sure, in the background, that we are already related, not as a nice idea, but really.

We are living as if we know the profound effect we have on everyone. The people we love, the people at work, the ones we relate with are affected, not by only what we do and say, but by our very vibration. Our being, our essential nature, and our heart is vital in our interactions.

What if human consciousness really does bring the world into being? This shift is like going from a flat world to a round one, from being the center of the universe, to a player in the mix of it all. It forces new thinking patterns. The old ones simply are ridiculous in terms of fixed people, fixed relationships, fixed ways of being.

Here is an example of the personal shift it would take:

The sun comes up and goes down. In our perceptions that is the way it seems to appear. We know in the intellect that this is not true. Remember Copernicus? He taught us this was false centuries ago. Yet, we still use these phrases and we still *see* the sun moving and we still behave as if it is, in fact, moving! Knowing the truth has no effect on our behavior.

How to honor the truth instead of perception?

To align with what is really happening, go outside and try this experiment: Look at the horizon. Gaze there and breathe into your feet, feel the beating of your heart relax your body. Let the eyes have a soft and wide gaze so that the peripheral vision is seen. Get still inside and you will feel the movement of the planet. With some practice, you will feel a shift in the body. It is exhilarating!

When you have been shown, by your heart and by your attention, that you are able to stand out and look at the horizon, let your perceptions fall away and you will experience the truth.

The way the world actually works is like this exercise. It goes against the senses. You need to expand beyond the senses into awareness to experience it.

This is what it will take. Our perceptions, through our conscious-ness, must change so that we can know the truth directly. The work of expansion will alter our awareness of relating. It will alter our awareness of belonging. It will alter our well-being and our fulfillment. It has the capacity to alter the very nature of who we consider ourselves to be.

In a vibrational view, we shift from a solid way of relating, where the goal is to know and understand, to a view full of change, uncertainty, awe, and wonder. The world opens up. It has more juice!

If we stay on the surface of life, we are frantically trying to figure out how to do life and relating. This takes a lot of energy. Expanded awareness lets us go beneath the surface of what is appearing in life to the deep currents. It lets us be in touch with that which has not yet appeared and is unfolding.

Beneath and through the deep current of life is our Source. Touching in with Source, with the Creator, we are all related. There we can live deeply. The movement of the hologram informs us, guides us. There we find faith that all is well.

"You can walk in the dream

in contact with the higher consciousness

that is the real you. It will find you.

You influence every event in the indefinite universe.

There is life in everything.

You are not what you have been taught.

Allow consciousness to unite with you."

-Anonymous

Readiness for a New Model

In our culture, we want fast answers and a quick fix. We want to be able to read about something or be told how to do something and, through that information, we will apply that knowledge to our actions and all will be well.

What is needed for relating in a different way is much more than acquiring more knowledge. What is needed is maturity, an unfoldment out of our stuck state, our stuck view.

First, we have to ask for the help of something bigger than our intellect. Next, we have to study how we, personally, are stuck. Then, we have to be expanded beyond our current view. Before we can set aside the suffering of the old view, the suffering that the old view has caused has to be healed.

There are several aspects to this healing. It includes being able to feel your own feelings in the body, as an experience, as well as coming to terms with the past. We do this not by avoiding the past, but by facing the pain and contraction of the past.

Y e s !	N o !
Introspection and self-examination	Self-incrimination and blame
Learn how to go through regret and remorse	Sinking into shame
Learn to have some mastery over the inner critic	Letting the inner critic win
Learn how to clean up the messes we have made	Harming others or us with our "clean up" methods
Learn to be alone in solitude, so our Creator can find us.	Always needing "noise" to comfort us

Yes!	No!
Learn how to get still, so we can hear the voice of guidance and regain our intuition	Drowning the voice of guidance with outside distractions
Regain our dignity and honor and self-esteem through forgiveness and grace	Being bitter and stubborn
Learn how to discern good people from bad people and good environments from ones that do not serve us	Repeating patterns that do not work. Continually placing ourselves in harmful and toxic situations
Learn to arrange our lives so we have a set of practices, individual to us, that keep us on our unfolding path *(One of these practices needs to be service and another needs to be gratitude)*	Complaining or waiting to be "saved." Being lazy

I know that this sounds like a lot of work and it certainly is if it were to be done entirely with the intellect. It would be slow and hard work. We can be thankful that we have lots of help in awareness, which is such a fast and effective teacher.

As far as I can tell, this is the work of being human. This is what is unfolding in all of us as we live. We do get stuck in some of the places as we mature. We want to stop along the way and live happily ever after and skip the lessons. The lessons get harder as we resist.

COMES THE DAWN

*A*fter a while
you learn the subtle difference
Between holding a hand and chaining a soul,
And you learn that love doesn't mean leaning
and company doesn't mean security.
And you begin to learn that kisses aren't contracts
and presents aren't promises.
And you begin to accept your defeats
with your head up and your eyes open
with the grace of a woman (or man),
not the grief of a child.
And you learn to build all your roads on today
because tomorrow's ground is too uncertain for plans
and the future has a way of falling down in mid-flight.
After a while you learn that even
sunshine burns if you get too much.
So you plant your own garden and
decorate your own soul
instead of waiting for someone to bring you flowers.
And you learn that you really can endure,
That you really have worth,
And you learn and you learn . . .
With every goodbye,
With every sunset,
Comes the dawn.

-Jo Anne Kurman

{PART TWO}

Touch and Go

Touch and Go
{ T H E   M O D E L }

The ***Touch and Go*** Model forms a living systems structure, so that relating can be conducted in a way that more closely aligns with the emerging world-view. This model takes into account a vibrant, dynamic, and alive view of the world.

Touch is the intimate meeting, the connection, which proceeds to closeness, which proceeds to Go. The Go allows for distance, and then intimacy can happen again, then closeness, distance, and again intimacy. It is a dynamic and fluid model, self-organizing and expanding. When you are in this dynamic dance, your development, your evolution, your expansion is exponential.

Go is separateness or distance, going inside, going back to center, and going to the psychologically distant position. Or, it can be going away physically. Psychological distance occurs when each person is centered.

When the system is looked at from an expanded state, it is the distance that allows for intimacy. Looking from the contracted state of the intellect, where our training resides, this concept is frightening. To the brain, distance seems like being cut-off or abandoned.

Distance is not negative. It is not the absence of closeness. <u>It is the reduction of involvement!</u> Distance can become negative when it is used to cut off, as in addiction, depression, rejection, objectification, fantasy, and ultimately suicide.

Healthy distance allows for many beneficial things. It allows for stimulus reduction and the resting of the senses. It allows time for self-reflection and meditation. It allows time for detachment, an escape into solitude and the chance to follow consciousness. It allows for the pursuit of solitary interests and to spend time with friends. It allows for time in nature and time with God. It allows for the shedding of stress.

Giving distance to another means maintaining separate physical space. It can mean the avoidance of eye contact. It allows for privacy and for separate possessions. It is a respect for timing and a respect for differences. It is not entering into the interior space of another person's psyche without their permission. It is keeping still and quiet and not having to fill space with talk.

If you stay in closeness and do not move apart, the energy is collapsed and intimacy's spark has no room to move between.

Again the pattern of the dance goes like this: distant or centered, move into intimacy, fall into closeness, move to distance or center again. These movements include all of the elements needed for a dynamic, self-organizing and expanding, changing system, a living system. This structure allows for the maximum development for those who are participating.

In *Touch and Go* relating, we are able to freely move back and forth between intimacy, closeness, and distance. The move to the center or distant position is important. It often takes great discipline to make the move away from closeness because closeness is so comforting. Too much time in the close position becomes toxic to growth and development. There simply is not enough room for energy to move through the system.

A sense of loss, pain, or fear of being alone can often accompany this move to distance. You can see why the real work of relating is <u>with oneself.</u> You need to have autonomy and know what center is. You need to be willing to be as comfortable there as you are in being close. If the nervous system is weak, if we are needy or unable to be alone, we end up grasping and upsetting the dynamic nature of the system. The system gets stuck.

BOUNDARIES

There are three important boundaries in **Touch and Go** relating: the personal boundary, the shared boundary, and the internal boundary of the system.

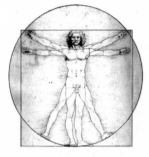

PERSONAL BOUNDARY

In learning to be separate, we have to become aware of our own energetic system. Leonardo di Vinci depicted this energetic system in his famous drawing of the naked man standing in a circle and a square. It is about as big as if you reached your hands out to the sides. It is like a big bubble. We call this energy field the psyche. It is the field that is used in the medical procedures called EKG, EEG, and MRI. In these procedures, even though the sensors are placed on the body, what is being measured is the vibrational field around the body, which is mirroring the activity inside. Or perhaps the body is mirroring what is happening outside? A phenomenon in the body is measured outside the body in the energetic field. What is going on inside of the body can be measured outside of the body!

Personal energy

Shrink-wrapped

Closeness

This system, this bubble of energy around us, gives us our own room or space to be, to look out from, and to rest in. We can look out from this steady place to study the world and our own responses. This is the place where we are centered, where we feel our own heart self, our own essence. We can feel it with our breath.

When we are afraid, this bubble contracts, it draws in, we become shrink-wrapped. During intimacy, this energy around us expands.

It can get very big—big enough to include the whole of creation where you are sitting in the heart of God!

During closeness, the energy around the two of you gets merged. This feels safer than the expanded state and that is why the movement back to your own energy field feels disruptive.

It is necessary, however, to move back to center because it is not only difficult, it is really impossible for the energy to expand again if you remain collapsed with another.

Autonomy is one of the most important ingredients for intimacy. This means that each person gets to have their own life, thoughts, feelings, preferences, ideas, friends, activities, time, and access to Source.

THE SHARED BOUNDARY

In the dynamic relating of *Touch and Go*, there is a shared environment with a fluctuating membrane or boundary much like a cell.

The boundary is negotiated and can include such physical boundaries as the place you live and how the living there will be conducted. It has agreed-upon behavior such as monogamy, telling the truth, keeping your agreements, being available, spending time together, and so on.

Time spent together helps form the boundary and so does keeping the agreements of the boundary over a period of time. You cannot hurry the development of the boundary.

The boundary sets up an internal environment. Inside is the shared environment for relating. A healthy, strong, safe environment provides a nourishing medium where each person can grow, and develop. The growing and developing people in turn strengthen the boundary and therefore the environment. You take care of the environment in which you have to relate and grow and the environment will take care of you. The quality of the boundary gets quite rich as the agreements are kept and strengthened with time. The number of rules diminishes as the heart takes over. There is a certain spirit of cooperation, honor, and trust that gets established and can be felt.

The environment contains an atmosphere where certain activities, occur and thrive and other activities are not tolerated. It is an environment free from addiction and violence or the threat of violence. The threat of violence is violent.

Each person makes certain they keep the agreements of the environment and that there are no leaks or breaks in the shared boundary, the shared place of relating. An example of a leak would be an affair, or too much time outside of the relating.

Inside the shared boundary, each person has their autonomy. They each have their own bubble of energy, their own space to be.

THE BOUNDARY BETWEEN

There is a third boundary in the *Touch and Go* system. It is a strong inner boundary between people that maintains the room for distance.

Within the shared environment there needs to be a very firm, clear boundary between people.

The boundary between consists of a respectful distance from the other person's life process. Uniqueness or separateness is necessary for intimacy. In minding our own business, we allow for connection, mutuality, and beloved Grace. As we reach across the boundary to take another person's inventory, or demand for them to fulfill our needs, we make a boundary violation.

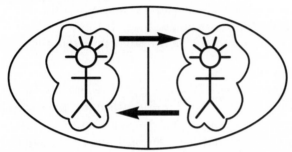

The boundary between can serve as a mirror. We have to stay on our own side and use self-examination and reflection. We have to stay involved in our own process in order to remain expanded. In the contracted state, we cannot share in another's world. We have no access to another person's vibration except through the heart in the moment of intimacy.

It is a boundary violation to tell others what they are thinking, how they are feeling, to give them advice, to have too much of our attention on them, to predict and anticipate what they will do next. It is impossible for us to know these things. It is none of our business and it diminishes them in our view to a thing, a machine that acts in automatic ways. Boundary violations like these are full of assumptions. We assume that they are not growing or in any way dynamic.

Other boundary violations include trying to fix them, to get them to do something to improve themselves, and gossiping about them to others. We are hardly ever right about others. Mostly, we are projecting our stuff onto them. We make a huge assumption about them even by using the word *you*. Mostly they will not listen to your view and will feel blamed. Your view of them is not true and it rips them off. You interfere with their self-examination, the room for them to see their lives for themselves, in their own way, and in their own time.

A blaming attitude is always lethal to intimacy and destroys closeness as well. It sets up a sort of false closeness, a view of them held in our head!

Keeping boundary is tricky and takes practice. We are so used to assuming and laying our assumptions on others. People have to be able to be responsive in their own life. We do not need advice from each other. Life is unfolding perfectly in each person's path. Another's path is none of our business unless in some way it is harming the shared environment. Even then, we need to use the skill of conflict resolution to resolve the problem without violating boundaries.

Boundaries provide safety. Structure gives freedom, freedom to be you, to learn, to let go into intimacy when it is present. Without boundaries, there is no register for the boundlessness, no place to return to after boundlessness contracts. Our brain thinks freedom is the free use of our will, so we reserve the right to exercise our will and avoid structure. Structure is the very thing that will allow for freedom.

The ego perceives boundaries and structure as domination or rules that limit our freedom. We follow the ego and avoid this suspected domination and then wonder why we are not profoundly related.

If you cannot be yourself, if you cannot stay centered while relating, there is often something off in the environment. There probably are not enough boundaries.

The boundary between is not unlike the distance that is present at the beginning of relating. Only now, there is the safety of the shared environment which has an energetic field of its own.

These boundaries bring to mind the image of nesting cups. A person's cells nesting in their organs, the organs nesting in bodies, bodies nesting in energy, energy nesting in a shared environment, shared environment nesting in community, community nesting in culture, culture nesting in the world, the world nesting in the universe, universe nesting in the heart of God.

In the *Touch and Go* model, you pay attention to two things:

1. **The environment in which each of you have to relate and grow and develop.**

2. **Your own growth and development.**

The boundaries dissolve in the moment of intimacy. However, until that moment, we must be able to maintain a dual awareness.

DUAL AWARENESS

Dual awareness is a skill that comes with an expanded state of consciousness. It is the skill of being with yourself and the other at the same time. You do not abandon yourself to be in the world. Being with your own heart, in your own essential self, while being related to another is the most important ingredient of the intimate experience. This does not mean only being with your thinking process, your personality, or your identity. It means including awareness, in the heart, with the breath.

USING THE BOUNDARY BETWEEN AS A MIRROR

This is an essential skill in dynamic relating. It is being able to use the boundary between people as a mirror. When we have too much attention on them, telling them what to do or how they are, our boundary violation is reflected and bounces back at us.

THEN WE GET TO ASK:

What am I avoiding in my life by having my attention on them?

What about them can I not tolerate in myself, in some form?

What am I unable to be with in them?

What do I judge to be wrong and therefore cannot allow for?

Who do they remind me of that I am incomplete with?

Finding all of this in myself becomes my inner work. Being related drives up our own incompleteness, our own unfinished work. We all contain the tormented, the tormentor, the murderer, the thief, the saint, the selfish, and the addicted. We may not be acting on these tendencies but they are latent in us and we are acting in ways that are irritating to others. The collective unconscious is moving through all of us.

Find these in your aversions. Find these in your desires. Find these in your dreams and nightmares.

Then we can go into solitude and examine our own reactions. As soon as we own our part and see how we get off center, we may share it with the other. This leaves us humble and vulnerable. It leaves us with compassion. It begins to become very clear that we act according to our own internal structure, our beliefs, our preferences, our training, our imprinting, and our past.

THE SOURCE OF WELL-BEING

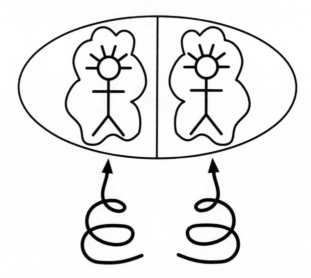

In the **Touch and Go** system, each person needs their own source of creative replenishment in whatever form is good for them. Getting source energy from each other will not work and will take away from the environment, depleting the energy. You cannot depend on another to provide your well-being, so stop demanding it. It is vital to allow yourself to receive this nourishment from Source and to allow another the same respect.

Life is difficult, so be in the source of rejuvenation often. Let yourself be refreshed and refilled.

This means that if the person you are relating with needs to be alone in nature several times a year or week to rejuvenate, you make certain you do not interfere. If your nourishment comes from going to church, you go, whether or not you have company. It is not necessary to have a shared source. Source comes to us in many forms. It isn't enough to know about God. We must know God directly.

INTIMACY

As trust and safety are established in the shared environment, and as you learn to return to center after intimacy happens, the opportunity for a more sustained intimacy is provided. There is the willingness to be swept into intimacy's vibration, carried away, losing the sense of being a separate self. Just before the boundary between comes tumbling down, there is a sense of dissonance. This is the ego's pause before the resonance, while the alchemy of Grace stirs the air.

Make friends with the fear of being lost; you are simply being transformed. Focus your soft eyes on the edge between you and the other and let God bridge the space between. You will be lost in splendor and lifted in expansion.

Structure dissolves with the arrival of Grace. Be swept into the heart and experience a meltdown of body, ego, place, time. Trust, have faith that you will be returned opened, greater than before you began.

Grace

Putting it all Together

Over the course of the past twelve years there have been many people who have taken on learning and living the model of *Touch and Go*. Each time there is a new dynamic, a new aspect that gets revealed. Here are some general descriptions of what emerges as learning grows and boundaries change and strengthen.

People have learned to ride the edge of the heart that allows for a deep sensitivity to the shared environment and to each person's autonomous space. They have learned to avoid leaning in too far toward another. Heart-centered attention also helps avoid leaning too far back from the other in isolation or being cut-off. The head does not have to figure anything out. The heart leads the way.

In such an environment, with shared safety and a clear boundary between, it becomes clear and joyous to dance between a joining together and a moving apart. There is a dynamic mix of centering, intimacy, closeness, and solitude that is alive and not predictable.

This becomes an environment where people are minding their manners. It seems that there is often a sort of formality that is really respect, honor, and trust. You can feel this in the atmosphere between people.

With such structure, you will find an easy, natural affection and delight. Goodness abounds along with dignity, kindness, and a deep love of creation. There is a sense of wonder and ease. It is a place of meeting together beyond words that is inclusive to others and feels warm and welcoming. There is an abiding gratitude spilling out into the atmosphere.

Here, there is a healthy conflict resolution process that is based on direct communication, and listening with the heart. When there is disagreement and upset, people look inside to figure out their part.

There is trust that resolution comes from an expanded state rather than from the intellect.

This is relating in a place where the wisdom of the heart reigns. A place where people who live there are carried on the wings of love to unspeakable heights of glory into the heart—into the hearts of each other and into the heart of our creator.

We intuitively know that all of this is possible. We have had glimpses of this expanded state. It is possible to have such intimacy, such an environment, within our own heart in our relationship with ourselves. In fact, this internal intimacy must be established within before it can be consistently experienced with another.

The Nature of Intimacy

Many of us can be centered, individualized, differentiated when we are not in a relationship, but as soon as we begin spending a lot of time with another, we become off balance, lost in enmeshment, emotionally and intellectually entangled, and pulled by immature expectations and desires.

In trying to attain the wished-for goal, each individual becomes out of balance, out of touch with his or her own sense of centeredness. When this happens, symbiosis and fusion or cutting off and aloofness become the only options.

It is strangeness, tension, and unfamiliarity that allows for the alchemy of intimacy. Martin Buber speaks of this in the book *I And Thou;* using phrases such as, "placing the other at a distance," "making the other strange."

Healthy relating does not mean togetherness. It is a dance back and forth, moving between intimacy and separateness, with closeness being a stage between the two poles. It is more like a trinity than a dichotomy.

When we are people who are dynamically and flexibly relating, we must be distinct, not enmeshed with the other. We must be able to have a sense of ourselves when we are alone or together. We must be able to know our own boundaries and principles. We must be able to withstand distance and be familiar and comfortable with our own emotional system.

Staying with ourselves needs to become the most important event in relating. Connecting doesn't mean feeling pulled off balance, off center.

It is important, essential to have personal space. We know this, but don't often honor it or allow for it. As we do our own inner work, we find out how the outer struggle is really inside of us. As we do more of the introspection and the self-examination, the outer struggles will disappear.

In our cultural training we have received some mixed messages. We are supposed to be individuals, but how to become ourselves is not taught to us. We are left feeling isolated and alone, relationally starved and needy. Being an individual without a Self is lonely.

On the other hand, our idea of being related is really a picture of enmeshment and symbiosis. We have ideas of being close, spending time together, reading each other's thoughts, fulfilling each other's needs. These expectations become the goals and this feels smothering, or at least falls short of fulfillment.

We often resent the misconceptions, the pictures, and the projections the other is carrying about us. But we hardly examine the assumptions we carry about them.

People are much more than their patterns, much more than their personalities or their tendencies. When we have experienced another directly through the heart, we have experienced intimacy. Intimacy is the most direct form of relating.

It is impossible to know someone completely—how they feel, what they think, or what they want. You can only know your idea of them, from history. We conveniently forget to remember that history is only our interpretation of events selectively remembered and held onto as truth.

This is second-hand relating. We must remain open and curious. We must be willing for the other to remain fresh and new.

The central problem is an insufficient relating with oneself.

When we have an insufficient relationship with ourself there is no center, no self-examination, no sense of our own core, our own tendencies and patterns. If we have no sense of our essential nature, which occurs in the heart, we have no availability for authentic relating.

Underneath a relational problem, there is often a personal problem. When we complain about people, complain about our partners, it is almost certain we would be having the same problem with anyone. The problem is internal, not external. We hardly ever think this.

When we are unhappy with ourselves, when we have unexamined qualities, hidden issues, and unfinished development, there is often suffering and unhappiness. This unexamined material, often called the shadow, is projected out onto other people with whom we relate. We accuse them of having bad qualities, but it is really our own unexamined qualities we are seeing out there in them.

Relating brings to the surface the best and the worst in us. It lets us know the unfinished parts of ourselves. As the old wounds get re-opened and played out with our partner, our associates, our children, we can continue to deepen and widen those wounds in each other, or we can learn to provide a common environment for healing.

If you hate yourself, you will find fault with the world and all those with whom you relate. Our image of ourselves is how we see all of humankind. How we view the world tells us how we see ourselves.

When we become willing to let go of our attachment to how we think things are, to let go of how we think we know the world to be, to let go of how we think people are, to let go of who we are, we avail ourselves of a greater experience.

We become ready to listen to our hearts.

We can learn to relate to how things are, instead of how we think they are or how we believe they should be. We can learn to differentiate fantasy from reality. We can learn to stop talking about relating as a way to relate. We can learn to stay still and notice the actual experience—learn to wait, to stay with ourselves, to be willing to join in our hearts with curiosity instead of knowing. We can be willing to stay in wonder and expectancy instead of expectation.

We can experience intimacy in another's presence and not turn it into a thing, not try to hold it or pursue it. We can be nurtured and changed by the touch of intimacy. We can settle into the sweet rest of closeness with gratitude for a time. And when that has also passed, we gladly go back to center so the touching has the room to happen again.

This is *Touch and Go*. We join with the nature of intimacy rather than the idea of intimacy.

"In reality

the only certainty

is in fantasy.

If you must have certainty

you sacrifice living."

-JB

First light, moon high, rustle

of wind, gently swaying Aspen.

Two standing parallel,

moving together in the breeze.

One stops and the other still moves.

They sway in opposite directions for a while.

One leans in toward the other, the other moves away.

Then suddenly in sync again.

There is a rhythm to relating.

Subtle, gentle movement,

apart, together, apart, together.

Depending on the movement of the whole,

the rhythm sometimes stronger,

the movement more gross.

★ ★ ★ ★ ★ ★ ★ ★

Become the watcher of the movement,

that which holds it all while

dancing this way and that.

That which holds it all is where

we stand in celebration.

Watching curiously with joy and wonder,

feeling the sway or the swing.

Deeply rooted and able to flex.

Knowing, sensing, becoming the rooting.

Never alone, subtly held,

rocked to the rhythm of the whole.

Tossed into the air, squealing with delight.

Thrust into darkness and fear.

With alertness finding light even there.

Relishing the awe of it all.

-JB

♥ ♥ ♥ ♥ ♥ ♥ ♥ ♥ ♥

Technique

We are now moving into the practical aspect of the ***Touch and Go*** Model. It is important to have a discussion about technique here.

Expanding beyond a particular view is often difficult, is often painful. There can be a great deal of loss associated with the shift. We would rather settle for the familiar. It is easier than the change that has to take place. We move away from expansion through many means. We dissociate, we distract, and we go into our compensatory behaviors. We do this because we are afraid. We are afraid of the unknown.

We all have compensatory behaviors that keep us from experiencing the full spectrum of life. A compensatory behavior is anything that keeps us from being present in what is happening before us right now. Planning, daydreaming, talking, checking out, asking questions, keeping busy, distracting, and so on are examples of these behaviors.

A weak nervous system or an untrained, undisciplined mind, along with fear of the emotions, can leave nowhere for the higher expanded states to be grounded. There is nowhere for them to register so that they can be noticed. We simply are distracted and not paying attention.

We must study and face the ways in which we avoid our own development, the places where we are uncertain and afraid.

One of our compensatory behaviors is to turn to using technique.

It is important to say a few words here about the danger of technique. Being taught through awareness and using techniques are two different things. You may use techniques to prepare yourself for being taught but the technique by itself will not give you anything. This is a very important distinction!

Many of us have learned technique and been very disappointed. We meditate, have good thoughts, do good deeds, eat vegetarian food, exercise, do affirmations, pray, do good works, and still we do not know intimacy. I have met many people in this inauthentic state. They are doing all the right things with no result. There are others that do none of these things and know the vibration of intimacy well.

An example of this problem is the use of vegetarianism as technique. To be a vegetarian requires a new view, a life-changing shift. I meet people who say they are vegetarian and what they mean is that they do not consume meat. This is far from being a vegetarian. In order to be a vegetarian you have to be eating vegetables, lots of them! That is how you receive enough nutrition. So we end up with people who are nutritionally starved, thinking they are doing a good thing.

We often get so focused on the technique that we are living indirectly, using only the logic of the brain without the reason of the heart. We end up performing our living, performing our relating.

We can move beyond techniques of the brain and be willing to be taught by the heart.

I am not saying technique has no value. I am just saying that technique is a vehicle, a map, a pointer, and not necessarily how intimacy will open for you. There is no one way. We all have to find our own way. So don't get hung up on technique.

Here is the test: any time we are comparing what is happening in the moment to how we think it should be, we are contracted into the intellect and we suffer.

We need to take our attention off the details in the foreground and move, in awareness, to the background, expanding as we wait there. We can be taken out beyond the plague of our culture. Out beyond the flat, uninteresting, repetitive, despairing, waking sleep.

"One of the reasons

we abandon ourselves as children,

or as adults,

is that we want love

and belonging so badly

that we're willing to do anything to get it,

and we are willing to abandon

ourselves in the process."

-Marsha Sinetar

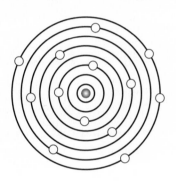

{PART THREE}

Inner Work

Self-Reflection and Examination

When we think of inner work, it may bring to mind mental work. This would be work done by figuring something out using the brain. The intellect is involved with inner work but the expression *inner attention* is a better way to indicate what will be leading the way. The intellect will always be thinking. We are not going to stop that. But eventually we want the thinker to learn to follow, rather than lead our life.

We have to be taken beyond the intellect, beyond our training, by first examining it. We have to see how it operates in us. This is the work of self-examination. In order *"to thine ownself be true,"* we have to study what we are made of. In this way, we can see the limitations of our view and find any mischief in it that is causing us suffering. We have to get honest about our insides in order to interrupt our projections and tendencies.

The most effective method for self-reflection and examination is to develop an observer. The observer is a tool of awareness. It is not a tool of the intellect. It is not cut off from what is happening. The observer remains detached, yet interested in what is happening.

OBSERVER

An observer is a part of your attention that watches what is going on in a mindful way. Here is an example of the observer watching.

Sleeping cozy, red dog beside, steeped in content, lazy, dozing, snuggled on the couch. Paw draped over the edge, chin there, too, breathing deep rhythms. My feet resting on her leg. The luster of the leg skin rich, slightly tanned. The shape pleasing my eyes, ankles firm flesh and perfectly stairstepped toes, relaxed at ease, content.

A catch in the hip, the dog adjusting, the scrape of her tough footpads on my ankle, not as pleasant as before. The sound of silence strong, not so much underneath now, singing in my ears. Remembering my sister, her planning, my joining in with that or instigating it? Trouble is all this planning that goes over and over in the brain. We are all a bit obsessive and compulsive. Stretch out this stiff, aching body. Feel its nature as it wakes for this day. Now noticing the background movement, the music of the trees. Itch around the eyes, on the edges of the lids, yawning, stretching skin of the lips, the ache of the catch in the hip, the urge to move, clenched jaw and the silence in my ears. Coolness on the legs and warmth on the back, another yawn. General ache across the back and dull ache of hunger stirring in the middle. Swishing cars along the road. Wonder what the day will bring?

As in this example the observer, our awareness is watching thoughts, body sensations, moods, and judgments. The observer is watching, observing, witnessing, and reporting what is going on. The best teaching book about the observer that I know is *Wherever You Go There You Are* by Jon Kabat-Zinn.

This observing is especially helpful and interesting if you remember to keep in mind that we are each living in our own subjective world.

IDENTITY

"*That I which is you my friend, does not consist in your body,*

nor yet in your soul, your consciousness, or your character.

You found yourself with a body, a soul, a character, as you

found yourself with the capital which your parents left you,

with the country in which you were born, and the human

society in which you move, just as you are not your liver, be it

sound or diseased, neither are you your memory, be it good or bad, nor your

will, be it strong or weak, nor your intelligence, be it acute or dull. The I

which you are, found itself with these physical or psychical things when it

found itself alive. You are the person who has to live with them, by means

of them, and perhaps you spend your life protesting against the soul with

which you were endowed—of its lack of will, for example—as you protest

against your bad stomach or the cold climate of your country."

-Ortega Y. Gassett

Who are we fundamentally? Let us begin by defining who we are not. We obviously are not our personality. We have a personality but it changes from situation to situation and from person to person and it somewhat changes over time as we mature. It isn't fixed. Even though certain tendencies are exhibited through our personality, such as being outgoing or withdrawn, friendly or aloof, these certainly are not all we are. So, we are not our personality.

We are not our feelings. This is a bit harder to get because our emotions are strong and exert their influence in a persuasive way. However, we could be injected with certain hormones called peptides and alter our feelings instantly. If you watch your feelings, you can tell they come and go with regularity. Feelings and emotions are fickle and so often are tied to circumstance following habitual pathways of behavior.

As we turn to examples set by mentors and those who have emotional maturity, we can see that they are steady and not so swayed by the coming and going of emotion. There is some skill they have. We can see that they have emotions but are not identified with them. Their emotions come and go and they remain at peace. This is because they are not following their emotions. The emotions are not suppressed or ignored but are simply passing through. It is quite clear from their example that we are not our emotions.

We are not our history. We have a history. These are the stories we think of and share about how we remember what has happened to us. Our account of an historical event in our lives is very precarious. The story may change depending on who we are telling it to and as we expand in consciousness, our interpretation of our past becomes more generous and expansive. In time, we can often see good in all that has happened. So we are not our history.

We are not only our body. We have a body but we are much more than just a body. When you look at a dead body, it is clear that the person is not in there. People who are physically challenged, like Stephen Hawking or Helen Keller, demonstrate to us that we are much greater than our body or its limitations.

We can get stuck in body identification, primping and re-arranging our presentation to be pleasing to others, to get attention. We lose sight that we are not our bodies. In fact, we will all get old unless we die first. We will lose our looks. In our American culture, this attachment to our bodies causes much turmoil. The advertising, cosmetic, dieting, and cosmetic surgery industries have all benefited from our compulsive identification of ourselves as our body.

We are not our thoughts. In fact, we do not even have our own thoughts. We live in a sea of thought. Carl Jung called this the collective unconscious. The same thoughts go through all of our minds. We do not all act the same or all follow the same thoughts, but we have access to all thought. If we put our thoughts on a loudspeaker, we would each be embarrassed. We are not our thoughts. Thoughts pass through us but do not identify us.

If we are not our personality, not our emotions, not our history, not our body, and not our thoughts, then who are we? Are we merely a collection of all of these? People have asked this question through the ages. Each of us has to find our own answer. The question, however, is an important one. The question is one that calls us to something higher. When we have found our identification with the vast nature of life in some personal way, then the grip of false identity weakens. We are left in the observation state. We can watch from detachment and enjoy the play of consciousness.

"First of all,

although men have a common destiny,

each individual has to work out

his own personal salvation for himself

in fear and trembling.

We can help one another

find the meaning of life no doubt.

But in the last analysis,

the individual person is responsible

for living his own life and for

"finding himself".

If he persists in shifting

his responsibility to someone else

he fails to find out the meaning

of his own existence.

You cannot tell me who I am,

and I cannot tell you who you are.

If you do not know your own identity,

who is going to identify you?"

-Thomas Merton

INNER CRITIC

We each have an inner critic. The inner critic is not the observer. The observer is neutral and merely notices, the inner critic is negative and often cruel. The inner critic criticizes everything. It is skeptical about life and other people. It is most active in putting us down and telling us how inept and stupid we are. Some people do not know that everyone has one of these inner critics. It is possible to think that this inner critic is you.

The inner critic can take over the mind. The negative self-talk can be a stream of unmerciful dialogue in the head judging everything. The inner critic is full of delusions and misconceptions about you. The harm and damage caused by these negative and cruel judgments is severe. It eats away at your self-esteem and can cause self-hatred.

It is possible to tame this aspect of the mind. First, instead of calling this inner critic "I", we give it another name. Giving it another name makes it possible to have some distance from it and begin to interrupt its hold on the mind. For instance, let us say you name your inner critic Howie. Instead of thinking "I am stupid and inept," you would think, "Howie says I am stupid and inept."

The second step in taming the inner critic is to study and learn about Howie. To change anything, first you have to identify it and recognize it and then you have to be with it. A way to do this is to use the observer. As the observer notices any negativity coming from Howie, you can write down all of the negative things that Howie is telling you. Slowly but surely, and sometimes very quickly, you will recover your mind. Truth will begin to challenge Howie and this inner critic will lose its power over the mind. Gradually, the influence of the inner critic can be eliminated.

It is important to purify the mind, for the future is determined by our present state.

The other day I was standing on a cliff overlooking the sea. It was cold and windy. I had gone there to express gratitude. I said a quick thank you in a cursory way and turned to leave when I heard a message in the mind. The message was, "Are you going to feel the

gratitude or just think it?" I stopped and turned back toward
the sea. I stood feeling the gratitude fill and move my heart. The
gratitude I had come to express magnified. It was a time of rejoicing
and celebration. In this case the inner critic had become my friend,
making a suggestion gently rather than shaming and chiding.

Learn not to let the inner critic pick on you. Do not let it cover you
with doubt. Learn to interrupt and correct the critic. The critic lives
in the ego. The frightened ego is making mischief, trying to keep you
small. Thank the ego for all it does well and gently let it know that
something greater is being invited to lead your life. The ego can rest.
It will be loved and can be useful. It just cannot lead the
way anymore.

STUDYING AND NOTICING

To study the world you are living in brings great insight and
guidance for living.

The intellect is an intricate system to ensure our survival, to sort
and classify, to learn and apply the learning. It is simply incapable
of registering the higher states of consciousness beyond the senses,
beyond mind.

Yet we are trained to honor only the intellect. We are trained into
limitation, scarcity, loss, and good and bad ways of behaving.
We are trained in objectivity and not the abstract. We honor logic
over reason. We step over the heart's intuition and vision.

All of our training has become more important than truth. The
subjectivity of the heart is ignored. Intuition is relegated to the
mysterious. We often override intuition in favor of logic. This
system of training and reactive patterns restricts the life force; it
blocks our way to expansion.

As you get used to examining and studying your life from the
point of view of the observer, you will expand your ability to find
your own wisdom in the heart. You will become tuned into the

body and all of its messages. You will become aware of the background and what is not being said and what is in between the breaths.

Along the path to wholeness, we have to eventually give up our intellectual and emotional attachments and identifications. Before we give them up, we have to know what they are. We study what they are with the observer.

The more we identify with our job, our roles, our opinions, our emotions, our personality, our history, our body, the more empty we will be. All of this, without heart and spirit, makes life dry and fixed and uninteresting.

As we ask to be prepared, we can ask Grace to work with us. We can ask to be shown how to notice. We can offer ourselves to have our consciousness expand.

Remember the instructions from the Bible: "Ask and ye shall receive." "Knock and the door shall be opened."

We can get ready to fly on the waves of ecstasy when intimacy is shown to us in the awareness of the heart. We can be ready to return to center when the grace-filled moment dissipates. We can be prepared to accept whatever comes next.

Our prayer could be that we be ready as Grace shows herself to us. We can ask to be there and ready, rather than distracted.

Our consciousness, our awareness, our heart, all are the expanding instruments that receive and enjoy intimacy's abundant Grace.

When we are not ready, when we are distracted by the world and we are not noticing, registering, and honoring the vibrations beyond the senses, we miss them. We are simply not tuned in to their frequency, the frequency that uplifts and carries us into the expanded states.

When we accept that intimacy is a gift, we can stop the pursuit of it, relax, and learn what blocks it in us. We can ask to be shown how to prepare and be ready to tune in. We can become vigilant and present in the observer state, developing discernment. Our nervous systems will become steady and strong with the ability to be in stillness.

The most important ingredient for intimacy is expansion, a life that includes the higher states of being.

This Matter of Being Alone

The fear of aloneness resides in the intellect. Because we are not trained or encouraged to learn about the expanded states, we are afraid. We call this fear, the fear of God. It is also a fear of the wholeness of life. We are afraid of the emotions, afraid of the negativity we might find inside, and afraid of our shadow nature. If we were not afraid, why would we have designed a culture that is based on the avoidance of anything negative and the relentless pursuit of pleasure?

We cannot do this work if we are afraid to be alone, to go inside. Loneliness is isolation. Solitude is the equivalent of alone in the higher states of consciousness; it is, however, the opposite of isolation.

To practice our inner work, we must be able to be alone. We must be able to go into solitude, instead of isolation. We can be in solitude in a crowd just as we can feel alone in a relationship. Solitude is sweet; it refreshes and fills us with the energy of creation. Solitude is full and deep. In solitude, we find an inner spring, an internal and eternal source, feeding us.

Go inside, be in solitude and let this Source of life fill you. It will spill onto others and the world. This is not something you generate. It is something you will experience when you get still enough to be tapped into it through Grace.

Contentment is based on truth, and truth is that it is impossible to be energetically isolated, truly alone. In the expanded state, all of life is included, giving peace, compassion, forgiveness, and room to belong. We must be willing to experience our own connection to the universal, in consciousness, through awareness.

The way to this kingdom is inside. The way to solitude, the way to awareness, is through the breath.

We are born in light, in the miraculous. We are enchanted, full of the life force, and vastly open, but we are trained to notice something else. We are trained by the culture into limitation, guilt, shame, scarcity, loss, and the *right way.*

We come into life alone and leave alone. All relationships end, some with leaving and some with death. Without facing this, we are unable to be truly related. We will have to cling to others or things, enmeshed and compromising our growth and development, our blossoming.

When we are afraid and withdraw from unfolding, we get stuck and attached. The avoidance of being alone causes distortions in our behavior.

Because we are afraid or do not know how to face this fact of life, we think a blissful union with another will save us. We hide in relationships or in the pursuit of relationship to escape our own aloneness, our unfinished pain, our unfolding development, and our own inevitable death.

We search for the soul mate, the one, a life partner. We want the end-all-trouble, fix-all-situation person to complete our life and enable us to live happily ever after. Instead, the venture often leads to happily hardly ever.

Our ideas of how we should be relating are unrealistic. Expecting relationships to fulfill us puts an extreme burden on another human. Human relating is not capable of delivering complete fulfillment.

We have a romantic dream for security and protection. We unconsciously search for someone to nurture us, care for us, for someone to depend on like a Mommy or Daddy, like a god in the form of a parent.

This fantasy, in the form of expectation, ideas, needs, and attachments leaves us trapped, caught in the tangled web of undifferentiated anxiety and fear.

We need to break with our dependence on the idea that anything on the outside will save us. We have to give up the quick-fix mentality or it will block our path, sending us in circular behavior, bringing disappointment, depression, and eventually despair.

So many of us are looking for *the one*. We mean the right one, a person, a soul mate. Perhaps the right one is within. Perhaps we are missing ourselves!

We can break this cycle of pursuit. We can save a lot of effort by realizing that every one is the wrong one. No one is going to be what you are looking for.

We have to finally get that we cannot have enough love and attention from another to make us happy. Fulfillment does not proceed from the outside. Happiness is an inside job.

We cannot be rich enough, good looking enough, smart enough, young enough, nice enough, good enough, charming enough, or famous enough to be rewarded with happiness or fulfillment.

We may have our yearning fulfilled by another for a moment, or an hour, or a day, or longer, but never forever. Human relating is not capable of complete fulfillment.

We are estranged from love, intimacy, and each other because we are estranged from life, from our hearts, from our own essential nature.

We want short cuts. We settle for the semblance of life and not the direct experience. We seek from another the love and caring we will not or cannot give to ourselves. We are missing ourselves. We have abandoned ourselves.

We are identified with our bodies, our personalities, our egos, our history, our stories, and our thoughts. We are unaware and out of touch with the essential being of our heart, our spirit, our soul.

We are unaware or have forgotten about the place of stillness where there is wisdom and eternal peace. The place where we will find abundant love.

Intimacy is apart from safety, a long way from being secure. That may be why we run from true intimacy, from the creator, from the mystery, from ecstasy. This place of intimacy that we fear so much is the very place where we must go to experience the connection we long for.

Intimacy is the only place to fulfill the yearning for union, the only place that will satisfy. Love is infinite, abundant, and inclusive in this place. We find this place in the subtle teachings of the heart where our true nature is registered and awaiting our recognition. There we will hear the still, small voice of our creator, guiding and loving us. We will be home there, belonging and free, confident and whole.

Usually, before we are willing to embark on the path that will allow for intimacy, we have to become disillusioned. We discover the outer search for well-being does not satisfy. We have to "hit bottom," have a broken heart, be seriously ill, lose a job, or be sick of too many serial relationships. Pain is a great teacher.

When we become disillusioned, when we have had enough of the repetitive cycles of old behaviors, beliefs, and happenings, when we become shattered by broken relationships, being abandoned, betrayals and disappointments, that is when we are usually willing to ask for help.

We have to get that we are trapped inside our patterns and habits and everything has become dull, flat, uninteresting, or worse. We have to understand that we are caught in the dramas of dire pain and emotional suffering and we cannot get ourselves out of the trap.

Hopefully, at this point, we will be given a teacher, a book, a mentor, a workshop, a friend who has gone before us on the path and can point the way. Hopefully, they point the way *inside.*

Here, a shift to the inner is needed. Something transformational is required.

The first step is admitting that what we have been doing is not working. This is the part that is like the twelve steps, where we admit we are powerless over how our relationships are going. We know that they are a mess.

We make a decision to ask to be fully functioning, a decision to ask to be moved from the concrete to the other state, the state of expanded awareness. We know that we will need a Higher Power to accomplish this, for we have tried and failed to get there by ourselves.

As we turn inward, we eventually learn that this powerful desire to merge with another is really a wish to merge with our own essential nature. It is a yearning to connect to our own divinity, the place of the heart where we are guided by creation, a place where we are never alone and always loved, One with the entire universe.

When we are brought to this place by Grace, the unconditional love we yearn for and wish to experience is found resonating within our own hearts.

We find this place, which is in all of us, when we dive inside. This is the secret place of the most high where love is infinite, abundant and inclusive. Intimacy abounds in this place. Our ability to receive this place and know it directly is the key to fulfillment. This is the place where we are able to tune into the hum of the life force.

Life is not the cause of distress. It is the absence of the expanded state, the absence of heart that distresses us. Not to know this secret inner place directly is the "dis-ease" of our culture.

How do we awaken to our own inner being? How do we find the edge of the unfolding into wholeness? Where are our teachers in this matter? When we have made the decision to be a traveler, how do we begin on the path?

How do we find this secret place inside? How do we move into this expanded awareness of the subtle heart nature? We have to develop the ability to be still.

After giving up the false dreams for fulfillment through our own efforts, we need to conclude that we cannot set out to make intimacy happen. Intimacy, expansion, comes by Grace without our effort, as a gift.

It is not generated in us but rather waits for us. We are the vessels of its expression. Our job is to stop seeking and prepare to receive the awareness of what is already there.

When the mind and heart are quiet, we can listen for the background, touch into the river of life force that runs through all, nourishing all, giving answers and guidance.

I know that this is an unpopular notion for the striving, doing brain, but it is true. Patience and asking are the keys to the opening of the door. Gratitude keeps the door open.

There is nothing to fear. You are not alone, have never been alone, and cannot be alone. Relax and explore!

"*It is not easy*

to find happiness in ourselves

and it is not possible

to find it elsewhere."

-Agnes Repplier

Becoming Whole

First, we become differentiated; then, we become whole. It is impossible to become whole without the first step of differentiation.

Becoming differentiated takes awareness, commitment, and focus. It requires learning. It requires being a student. It requires being teachable.

Before we are differentiated, we are enmeshed. Enmeshment is a bit like pea soup. If you have ever made or had pea soup you know that there are many ingredients—peas, carrots, ham, onions, garlic, salt, pepper, celery, and sometimes potatoes. Some people eat their pea soup with all the ingredients intact, but many times the ham bone is taken out and the rest is put in a blender and pureed. When that happens, you can no longer tell where the peas are, where the carrots are, and so on.

Enmeshment or nondifferentiation is like pureed pea soup. You are lost in a fused system and have lost your own identity. You are no longer different or differentiated from the rest of the system. You have no boundaries of your own. In pea soup, the blade of the blender is the device that keeps the system fused. This blade, in an enmeshed system, consists of guilt and shame, sameness, envy, fear, and sticking together.

In an enmeshed system, there are unwritten agreements that no one can rise up any higher that the rest of the system. No one can be successful because someone else might feel bad. For example, when you come home with good grades and your sibling has not, no one gives you acknowledgment for the good grades because the sibling might feel bad. Or you are brought down to the level of the system through irony or shame. For example, you are told that you are too full of yourself, too cocky or conceited.

A fear or absence of intimacy often has its roots in our families of origin. Our families were either too close or too distant. Take your roots out of your family of origin and give them to God. Take your roots out of society. The more you identify with any aspect of society, the more dependent you are. In order to differentiate and become a Self, we must psychologically, emotionally, and sometimes physically break loyalty with this system. We have to be willing to break our belonging to such a system and give ourselves to something higher.

We have to give up our identification or our belonging with the family of origin, the dysfunctional workplace, or our primary relationships. Our primary relationship will shift to belonging with humanity or the universe or whatever vast description appeals to us. This does not mean that we give up our participation with these people or stop loving them, but we stop having them be so important in our life. We give up having what they think is important, determine what is important to us. They are not the primary focus. If we find that any of those systems or people are not good for us, we become willing to leave them behind and instead be open to unfolding.

We become free to study and learn. As a student of life, we will learn what it means to be true to the Self.

- Learn what distracts us.

- Learn our own tendencies and patterns.

- Learn the difference between intellect and awareness and how that feels in the body.

- Accept the training of the mind.

- Learn to move beyond emotionalism to feeling and honoring the deeper, more subtle, intuitive emotional states where wisdom comes through the heart.

- Learn the difference between logic and reason (one suppresses and disregards emotion, the other is informed by the heart's deep subtle emotion).

- Learn to respect what is happening in the environment including how environmentally and culturally sensitive we are. This means the physical environment and also the atmosphere or feeling in the air.

- Learn to respect and notice what is happening between people.

- ✓ Learn to imbibe wisdom rather than trying to live a good life.

- ✓ Learn eternal values and principles for living.

- ✓ Learn stillness.

- ✓ Learn respect for process, the unfolding nature of consciousness, patience.

- ✓ Learn soft focus so that part of our attention is on the background, between thought, between actions, and between breaths.

- ✓ Learn to separate the still, small voice of spirit from the confusion of the collective thoughts burping up in the mind.

The name of the game is to wake up and remember our original state. In Sleeping Beauty, the prince, our *animus*, goes through the brambles to find the princess, our *anima*. Together they become One, the true essential Self and live happily ever after. They live in an expanded state, eternally detached from the trouble of the world.

How do we find our way back? We find our way by examining our patterned ways of relating and living. We have to become disillusioned with the status quo. We must give up our romantic illusion, which comes from the fantasy of the culture. We have to become willing. We have to be willing to give up our projection of our tendencies onto others. We have to be willing to grow out of the contracted state of thinking into the expansive nature of the heart.

Becoming a whole human being means not fearing our own energy, being able to keep a center in the midst of emotional turbulence. We must be able to keep our own rhythm in the midst of the distraction of the world. We must be able to be close and distant, intimate and dissonant.

To become a whole human being means to have our own energy system separate from other people. It means we know our own uniqueness and the ways our emotions are triggered and register in our system. It means we are aware of our own thinking process and have learned not to speak or act on all the thinking that travels through our system, not to act on every emotion. Unchecked and unacknowledged emotion has devastating effects.

In a mature person, a whole person, there is a certain psychological emotional health. We know at this point in our development that we have emotions, we are not identified with them. Our thoughts and our emotions happen, they are not who we essentially are. We are beyond emotional dependence. We are steady and true to our Self no matter what is going on.

A whole person is principle based and is not resisting the present. This person makes no demands on life to be different than it is. This person has given consent for God to enter, to expand, and to lead. This person knows that there is a combination of grace and self-awareness that leads to fulfillment. We cannot just wait and we cannot just work. There needs to be both.

A whole person is in contact with their inner spirit and has an inner sensitivity to the natural rhythm of life. They embrace and invite change as the only certainty of life. They care deeply for others, are eager to hear, are accepting, and fully present.

A mature person knows that people are brought in and out of our lives. Some stay for a lifetime and others only for a while. Those who have touched us in the heart stay there in the heart's memory and are therefore always with us. We might as well bless and forgive those who we consider to have harmed us, otherwise the heart remains constricted. A whole person can accept misfortune.

Suffering is okay, depression is a great teacher. Staying centered and flexible through it all is our great task. Be where you are. If you are contracted, be contracted and if you are expanded, be expanded. Notice what there is to notice. Interact with what is in front of you. Life is quite simple, really!

The required skill for intimacy is to be human. The required skills for plenty of intimacy are having autonomy, being able to tell when you are off, knowing how to get back on, being okay with the dissonance, okay with all of life, and having faith.

Two important distractions are the material world and taking credit. When we fail to give the credit and the thanks to Spirit and think that we are doing it all, somehow life dries up.

When we are whole, we are aware that we are not done, not finished. Growth and development and spiritual maturity are lifetime events and we accept this gladly. To be alive and whole is to be changing.

We are productive and creative.

We serve others.

We are spontaneous and open.

We admit when we are wrong.

We take good care of us.

We have a mind of our own.

We are true to what is happening within us.

We are guided from within.

We have confidence.

We don't have to conform to the world.

We learn.

We love.

"How Might I Serve?

For I am so served

So loved

So elevated

So clear

So utterly safe

So held

So cared for

So fulfilled

That I overflow, exuding forth

I run out onto all encountered

I receive

Therefore I serve"

-JB

An Expanded Center of Consciousness

Underneath all of this teaching and learning there is a greater center of consciousness that lives everywhere, lives in all the contraction and all the expansion of life. It lives and is accessible inside your body, heart, mind, and consciousness through awareness.

This center does the work of the body without your help. This center is very, very, very fast. It is much faster than the intellect. Can you imagine trying to run the functioning of the body with the intellect?

This higher center is in the vast nature of higher consciousness, accessible through awareness. Awareness comes in the silence by Grace and is subtle. It is a sort of wordless sensitivity, a direct sort of natural knowing that happens before word, before thought. It has a register in the body. We often feel it during the experience of intimacy.

It is everyone and everything's authority. Find your own inner authority. It is not in your head. The brain is not designed to go to expanded levels of awareness. These higher levels are neither concrete, measurable, nor do they register with the senses.

There is a field that surrounds us and moves through us. It contains the wisdom of the ages. It is available. As we experience our connection to this universal spirit, this vast consciousness, we expand and meet it. This is the experience of intimacy. Great teachers and great wisdom through the ages have shown us the way to this expanded, heightened state.

Wise teachers will not answer our questions directly but will point the way. They will direct us inside.

Getting Still and Getting Present

As we are awakened in consciousness, we become more fully ourselves, more expansive, inclusive, full of wonder and awe and gratitude. We are more open to the mystery of life.

To overcome the distractions of the world it is necessary to practice, to tame the mind, and strengthen the nervous system.

When we do not do this, we may be left with an idea of the divine and miss the experience of the divine. We cling to our ideas of the mystery, of our creator but become largely afraid, unwilling, or untaught how to access the mystery directly.

In teaching handed to us from the past, through the lives of the saints and mystics and in the sacred texts, we are directed *inside* to find the truth.

This does not mean inside our heads, for that is not where truth abounds. Inside is more in the region of the heart and body, found by traveling with the breath.

Meditation is the best method for liberation and training of the mind. It also strengthens the nervous system. It is possible for all of your consciousness to be purified in meditation. As more and more gets released from the unconscious, as the purification process of meditation occurs, there are fewer ripples on the surface of the mind and we reach the wisdom place. Meditation combined with self-examination or psychotherapy can hasten the process.

If we were to measure your brain waves using an EEG, or electroencephalograph we could map out different states by the brain waves.

(see chart on the next page)

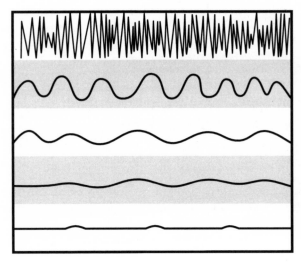

Agitated State
(High Beta)

Ordinary Waking
State
(Beta)

Relaxed State
REM sleep (Alpha)

Referred to as the
Meditation State
(Theta)

Hibernation State
(Delta)

It is important to remember that any of these brain waves can occur naturally during meditation. Because we have been trained in such a goal-oriented thinking system, we tend to focus only on achieving a theta state. We are discouraged and disappointed when we cannot make it happen.

I like to think that whatever happens during meditation is none of my business. Meditation is the time of the day that I offer myself to meditation to do its work with me. Meditation is very powerful. It will clear out old patterns and tendencies without the help of the intellect!

Meditation is the most important inner work that you can do!

To MEDITATE:

1. Sit in a quiet place, if possible. Meditation can happen anywhere but fewer distractions are helpful as you are learning.

2. Sit daily in the same place, at the same time, if possible.

3. Give yourself to meditation.

4. Give up the right to vote or judge your meditation as good, bad, difficult, right.

5. Put your opinions aside or let them pass by and let meditation have its way with you.

6. Sit with your spine straight, erect. Do not lie down because this is a signal for the body to go to sleep.

7. You may fall into a sort of sleep during meditation but it is different than ordinary sleep. I like to think that this is meditation's way of turning off thinking long enough to work with you without its interference So if you fall into this kind of sleep, don't worry.

8. Make sure your body is comfortable. If you sit in a chair have both feet flat on the floor.

9. Close your eyes and put your attention on the breath going in and out of your nose. Find the place at the nose where you can feel the breath and focus there. Follow the breath.

10. When you notice you are distracted, gently come back to the focus. After some minutes of concentration at the nose the mind will naturally shift into a deeper state. You'll be able to feel this. If feels like part of the body beginning to get heavy. Some feel it in their hands and some in their legs or their trunk or throughout the body. As you feel this shift to heaviness you can shift your attention from the breath at the nose to the heaviness and pleasant feeling spreading in the body. Stay focused on this pleasantness and the mind will naturally shift itself into a happy and joyful place.

11. Stay focused on the joyful heart and the mind will shift to calm. Stay with the calm and you will shift to a vastness or expansive, quiet place where you will lose awareness of the body or thoughts. Rest there.

12. Attention on the breath can be your focus. You may also want to use a mantra or word to focus on. As in the Christian practice of contemplative prayer, you can choose to use a sacred word, one that has meaning for you, such as joy, love, peace, and so on. You repeat the sound or word inside your mind until it takes you into a deeper state. Other Sanskrit words can be repeated such as om or so-hum. The attention, or mantra, or sacred word is the vehicle into the other states. It is not the goal to be repeating this for the entire meditation.

13. The mind is fickle and vigilant, constantly scanning the environment to make sure we can survive. It is very good at this but does not know how to shut itself off. During meditation, every time you notice that the mind is doing its distraction thing, you simply and gently return to your focus. Go back and back to the breath, to your focus. Go easily, without judgment for having been distracted. It is not bad or wrong to be distracted. It is part of the process. So when you are distracted, easily and gently move back to the breath.

Lots will happen in meditation—you pay attention to the breath. Each time you catch the mind wandering and bring it back to the focus you are building your practice, you are taming the mind and strengthening the nervous system. When at first you are aware of noisy thoughts, this means you are getting quieter and the ability to notice is being strengthened.

Waves rise and fall back to the ocean. So do thoughts and emotions and body sensations. Let them go by and you stay with your focus. The breath, or the mantra, or the sacred word will take you into calm. Or you may stay agitated and distracted the whole time you are sitting. If that is happening, keep sitting. Eventually, over time, the mind will settle.

Remember that sometimes in meditation the mind remains active or agitated. Let it be this way and just sit. Sometimes the mind will go to the more restful state of alpha, where the breath is slower and thoughts are fewer. Sometimes the mind will go to the even deeper state called theta. The reason most people call the theta state meditation is that thought mostly disappears at this vibration. In the even deeper state of delta, the breath hardly comes at all. This is good to know about because it can be surprising when you find yourself in this place. The Delta state is the vibration where animals exist when they hibernate. Everything is slowed way down.

During any meditation, you may experience all the states. It doesn't matter what states happen or what you think of the meditation. Please, just sit each day.

Release the thoughts that take you to trouble and release the ones that take you to pleasure. Stay with the breath. The breath will take you inside to the heart of the essential Self.

Go back to the breath each time that you are noticing anything. When nothing is happening, that is fine. The moment you notice activity, go back to the breath.

It can feel vulnerable to be sitting with your eyes closed, especially at first when you cannot feel your own energetic system. You can wrap yourself in a blanket, which offers a container.

Meditation will clear out the receiver, the body, and the mind. Train yourself to get still. Find out how to stay clear and in your center without following every thought or emotion. Have the thoughts and emotions, yet do not follow them into action or musing. Keep your center, stand your ground and you will be given the opportunity to respond rather than react to life. You will be able to stay with what is presented instead of being pulled off center by your tendencies and expectations or the wanderings of the mind.

Without a listener, the music of life dissolves. It abounds yet is unnoticed. Without a listener, the bountiful resonant glory of life melts into all, waiting to come again and again and to eventually fall upon an open heart, a listening heart.

Will you be able to hear?

Dealing with the Emotions

We have to ask to be shown our essential self, our heart nature.
We have to plow through the brambles of our unexamined life.

When we have found and developed an observer, we can learn intense
introspection instead of self-blame. We can get curious and observe
all sorts of things we formerly thought were our identity. We observe
our personality and find it interesting. We observe our actions, our
motivation, our opinions, our thoughts, our feelings and emotions,
our judgments as interesting phenomena. We become more and more
identified with our observer than with that which we are observing.

In order to get the emotions purified, so pure that love can register,
we have to face them, move with them, and hear their message.
There are two distinct kinds of emotions. There are those that
register in a gross way in the body. These gross emotions are
dramatic and you know they are occurring. These include grief, fear,
anger, jealousy, anxiety, happiness, excitement. There are more subtle
emotions that register more in awareness without the acknowledgment of intellect. These more subtle emotions include intuition,
wisdom, compassion, bliss, and joy.

The gross emotions are those we think ourselves into. These are emotions
that happen because of an external stimulus like a movie. Then there are
the spontaneous emotions that begin in experience. The spontaneous
emotions move up in the body and the others come down from the head.

Even though we know that we live in a world that exhibits an entire
array of emotions, we do not often include all of them in what we feel.
We shrink away from some of them. The trouble with this approach is
that the more you cut off from the negative emotions, the more
vulnerable you are to being taken off center by them when they occur.

We can learn to deal with all of the emotions without being carried
away from center. This is accomplished with a certain detachment. It
is not closed down against the emotions, not cut off, but observing
them with awareness, in the breath.

Our training is to view the emotions as confusing, frightening, and a nuisance. We call it *breaking down* when we cry. We believe that if we experience the full range of emotions we will become crazy or lost in them and not come back.

In our attempt to control the emotions, we limit the breath. In holding the breath we don't feel emotions, we suppress them. Later those suppressed emotions may erupt in violent outbursts or leak out onto others and into our lives, coming forth at odd times.

As we fear the emotions, we tighten against them, causing them to get stuck. When we turn away from our emotions, we cut ourselves off from important information and guidance. We are left with only the intellect to deal with life and this is not enough!

I am not saying we should act out the emotions. I am saying we should feel them. We can learn the skill of transmuting the emotions, to release their wisdom, letting them pass through the system. This skill is learned by expanding awareness and registers in the awareness.

When we receive an emotion we can ignore it, distort it, project it, deny it, or welcome it and receive its message. We can learn to let the emotions speak to us. The emotions, their movement and sensations in the body are the messages of wisdom.

Transmutation is like finding the edge of a wave in surfing, the balance point of a bicycle, the edge as you ski downhill, or the edge of a contraction during childbirth. The emotions have an edge, too. We find it in the body. Learn to lean into the edge of the pain, the anger, the grief with your attention and your breath. Ride the edge with the breath until the emotion releases its message and the bodily sensations subside.

If we can lean in and study that which traps us, we have expanded to include the trap and are no longer caught. This movement in awareness will open us. Going toward the emotions, facing their vibration, releases their message. We are left with guidance.

Feel the nature of the emotions, the texture, the movement, rather than suppressing them, manipulating them, or acting them out. Go into the darkness and with your higher power heal the pain and purify the system. There is a pool of well-being under the trauma of our lives. This pool contains all the wisdom of the ages. It is pure and untouched by trouble and hardship. It is free and expansive beyond what we can imagine with our brain.

Go inside and meet it there. The path out of the quagmire of the mind is filled with the trials of distraction, so this will take some focus. The more we let ourselves go into the vibration of an emotional disturbance, the more we become aware. In awareness, transmutation manifests and the turbulence is stilled.

We are very busy, collecting things, having too much attention on other people, having too much attention on the world. We overeat, over-stimulate ourselves, and watch too much TV or too many movies. We overwork, ignore our own signals, our bodies, our cravings for truth. We talk too much, think too much, drink too much alcohol, use drugs, shop till we drop, sleep, and have serial relationships.

We are hardly ever still. Our creator cannot find us!

Stop distracting! Stop saying there isn't enough time. Join the life force; join life, real life. Accept your inner self just as you are, get still and listen to your own vibrations.

Say yes! Yes to feeling it, to having all of the emotions, to letting the life force inform us and change us, carrying us into the depths of despair and longing and up to the heights of the sublime.

Coming to Terms with the Past

As we work with the obstacles that interfere with fully living our lives, we will come to terms with the past and know how to do this on an ongoing basis. We will study our own training and imprinting, our own propensities.

We will learn that we have and have had little control over what has happened to us in our lives. We will learn that we do have something to say in the interpretation of what has happened. We can stay in contraction, holding on to disempowering stories of the past, or we can learn to interpret them powerfully, accepting our predicaments as teachings, therefore coming into compassion with our perfect unfolding. We can learn to attend to the neglected part of ourselves and provide the soothing it needs to heal.

We can learn to include all that occurs along the path to wholeness as experience to savor and move through instead of something to judge.

We cannot, however, skip the process of going inside to clear out the past. What will we find when we go inside? We will find the demons of unfelt life. We will meet the unprocessed, suppressed horrors of our life; the pain we have put away is there. We will meet understanding and wisdom and self-acceptance and love. We will find it all.

We belong to the whole of life, to humanity. We are all largely the same. I have not met anyone who has not had some sort of suffering. We have the same trials, the same troubles in different form. Some are better at hiding it and some are better at coping with it than others, that is all.

We come with fear, anger, sadness, grief, and love. We learn help-lessness, isolation, embarrassment, and shyness. We learn shame. Each of has habits and grooves in the psyche. We all have *stuff* to work with.

You can be transformed by coming to terms with the past and the renewal of the mind. So feel the pain, dissolve into it, feel its aliveness, find its message. The pain will open you, leaving you wiser and changed.

You can meet past troubles in awareness, on the edge with your breath. There at that edge they are transformed through the alchemy of grace, expanding our consciousness in the process. Awareness is very fast, much faster than the intellect. Awareness through subtle attention gives you sensitivity. We pick it up with the breath before words. Put all of your attention on the breath and dive inside. Meet what is waiting to be healed and claim what is waiting for you there.

When you don't like what is happening, be with it in this way until it expands you enough to be included. Stretch! Do this with the breath. All suffering is thinking that things should be different than they are. Remember that life should not be different than it is. Let life's challenges unfold you. In the expansion of consciousness and of one's own sense of the expanded states, everything becomes inclusive. All of being human is included, giving peace, forgiveness, compassion, and room to be.

Sit with anger, sorrow, hatred, jealousy, fear—all the things you think are negative. Focus on the body sensations with your inside attention on the breath. If you become lost and desperate, begin to look in the background, slow down, stay inside. Stop judging. With the breath, find the vibration rising up through the body into the chest and the mouth. Look up with the inner invisible eye and make your mind soft. Gaze at the periphery. From this place, allow the grace in the life force to fill you and rinse you clean of trouble.

As this source fills you, it will spill out, healing your life. Your heart will be flooded with love. This is not something you generate but something you receive. You get it through Grace when tapped into higher consciousness.

To discern between the heart and the head, you have to join the breath. When the mind and the heart are quiet, one can listen for the background. We can step into the river of the life force that runs through all, nourishing all, giving answers and renewing us through the breath.

Reducing our emphasis on the appearances of life, we turn inside and find the inner kingdom, full of majesty and glory, expansive and inclusive, reaching out to include the mundane and glorify it.

As the mind is tamed and your tendencies diminish, happiness moves in. The clouds can come and go, leaving us content.

A Set of Practices

Since structure is what provides freedom, it is important to have a set of practices in our life to help give us a structure along the way. This set of practices is very personal and can change over time. The most important practice is some form of getting still and getting quiet.

Going inside and checking in is a practice. Resolving the past as it comes up is a practice. Eating so that your body can remain steady is a practice. This includes making sure your hormones are balanced. Out-of-balance hormones can cause emotional havoc. Exercise and staying healthy and well is a practice, as is getting enough rest and relaxation. Making a home warm and comfortable and beautiful and safe is a practice.

Spending time in nature is an important practice for many. When we are in nature, our bodies align with the vibration of nature and we feel expanded. Prayer is a practice. Meditation is the highest form of prayer, for in meditation we are receptive and listening. The conflict resolution exercise that comes later in the book has become an important practice for many people. Having part of your awareness on the breath and breathing down into the belly is a practice.

Solitude, contemplation, and study are helpful and, for many, necessary practices. Music and art and sports can lead to a heightened state of consciousness. Having a mentor or teacher or guru is a powerful practice. Hanging out in good company will also work!

Any set of practices you choose should include:

• Feeling your own feelings in the body
• Coming to terms with the past in an ongoing way
• Doing your inner work
• Allowing for the experience of God
• Maintaining the practices

Your set of practices will ensure that the mind is disciplined, that you get strong, that you are in touch with yourself and the subtle emotions, that you have reason beyond logic, that you are able to stay in your center no matter what life delivers to you.

Communication

Communication is not an action; it is a place in consciousness. Communication is not about words, even though words may be present. Communication doesn't necessarily need words. The words are embedded in context and that context is in the unsaid. It isn't the words that convey the meaning. Under the words there is a current, a vibration that carries the understandings. Communication is about being connected. It is the process where you find yourself in communion with another. You can be in communication with someone when they are not even present.

Communication is not agreement. Many couples complain that they don't communicate. They are communicating just fine. What they really mean is, he/she doesn't agree with me.

Communication is being with another while something unfolds between you. When our vibrations are aligned, when we are tuned in, communication is happening without our effort. When we are "out-of-sync" or off, our vibrations are dissonant and there is no alignment and no synergy. Since the world is in constant flux, resonance goes in and out.

Learn to be with the flow, have patience, stay with the dissonance until it returns to resonance again. When things get hard, stay in the dissonance. See the hard times through. Stop achieving and live.

We think if we are not in communication there is something wrong with the other person or with us. We do not wait. We move into trying to make something happen. This is always a mistake.

For a safe environment, for effective communication, we need freedom and limits. We need to know how to be clear and direct. We need tolerance for differences, we need to make room for each other's tendencies, we need limits of acceptable behavior, we need mutual goodwill, and we need to learn the art of "I messages." We need to modulate and transmute the emotions and not cloud the environment with anger and frustration. We need to know how to compromise without hurting ourselves. We need to know how to give information without blaming another. We cannot be putting ourselves or others down. We cannot interfere or interrupt or change the subject to avoid conflict. We cannot lecture, get intellectual, and discount another's feeling. Everyone gets to count.

We need to know how to deliver emotions honestly and not withhold. This does not mean we say whatever crosses our mind. It means we learn to monitor our own process so that we can express ourselves without demeaning another. With respect for our own internal state, we tell about the condition of our inner world.

LISTENING

"*Let me give a little hint on how to listen.*

The point is not to listen to a series of propositions,

but rather to follow the movement of the showing."

-Martin Heidegger, On Time and Being

It is impossible to listen when we already know. Our attachment to already knowing is very powerful. When we listen on the surface, for knowing, we listen through the old view.

We listen for knowledge.
We listen to gather evidence for what we already know.
We listen for content.
We listen to be polite until it is our turn to speak.
We listen for what we disagree with.

True listening does not occur in the mind. It is effortless. When the mind relaxes, when you are present, when you are listening with honor and curiosity, listening for letting things in, it is soft and expansive.

The most respectful gift we have to give another is to listen to them directly, with our reactions and judgments suspended. When we let our reactions and judgments go by, we can stay with the other.

We can experience all of each other, all the goodness and all that we find displeasing. We can learn to listen for letting things and people be.

When we do this for another, hopefully they will be as generous with us. We can only offer this type of generous listening if we are aware of the workings of our own mind and emotions. It is in awareness that we are allowed to take a step back from our reactions and be open. When they are finished speaking, it is best to pause and let things settle, simply finding a way to say thank you. This is because when someone shares with us, it is sacred.

Having part of our attention on our own heart, our own essential nature while being with another is not selfish. It is a requirement! Never does being helpful or critical result in connecting. Listen with them.

Speaking

Mostly we talk to fill space because we are uncomfortable with silence. How we speak is a reflection of how we see ourselves. If we speak too quietly to be heard, it is because we do not think we are worthy of being heard. If we speak loud and with force, it is because we are unsure of what we are saying and covering it up. If we are blaming others, it is because we are setting them up to be defensive and we make sure, in that way, that they cannot hear what we are saying. Then we get to be right about how they do not listen.

When you go inside and get still, you will know what to say. You will say what wants to be said in the moment, not from memory or technique. Your speaking will be connected with the context of the background. It won't sound hollow and inauthentic.

When speaking isn't flowing, when you are not being given what to say, then say little. Learn to wait with another. Say in those times only what is kind, true, and necessary.

When we superimpose our will and our timetable on another's process and urge another to speak before they are ready, we will be sure to have them resist or counter what we say. We often use the word *you* followed by our opinion. It sets them up to be defensive.

There is no list, no right path, no technique, no answers or solutions, no doctrine, no rules for right behavior. There is only the heart, and the guidance that comes from there. Find the heart and follow its guidance.

"*It is not necessary to always think* **WORDS.**

WORDS *often keep me from acting in a fully intuitive way.*

Fears, indecision, and frustration feed on **WORDS.**

Without **WORDS** *they usually stop.*

When I am trying to figure out how I should relate to someone,

especially a stranger, if I will stop thinking **WORDS,**

and listen to the situation, and just be open,

I find I act in a more appropriate,

more spontaneous, often original,

sometimes even courageous way.

WORDS *are at times*

good for looking back,

but they are confining

when I need to act

in the present."

-Hugh Prather

ANGER

In open and honest communication, we speak our truth in the moment. When we withhold, we are really protecting ourselves from what we assume the response will be. Give up your need for agreement. Stop moving away from conflict. Learn how to have conflict and it will enhance your relating.

There is strength in dissonance. In dynamic relating, disagreement is good. Usually, we will move into anger to avoid dissonance. We hardly ever tolerate the unsettling vibrations of disagreement and let things work out. We don't trust the system. We want to force resolution.

There are productive forms of anger and damaging forms of anger. Anger used to manipulate or threaten or intimidate is intrusive and therefore violent and disrespectful. An environment where anger is in the air is toxic.

The right use of anger is to recognize it as a signal. It usually indicates that there is something amiss in the environment. We either need to set a boundary or leave the atmosphere of the environment.

As soon as you feel anger rise in the body, meet it with your breath. Find its warning, and respond rather than react. There are four major kinds of anger. There is violent anger that intrudes into another's container and is destructive. There is anger that sets an immediate boundary such as, "Stop!" or "I will not put up with this," and is productive. When we are not able to feel our anger and set boundaries, the anger often simmers inside and can turn into self-blame and negative self-talk, and of course, this is unhealthy. Again, the healthy use of anger is to see it as a signal that something is off in the environment and we need to set a boundary or leave.

Do not use the anger to set a boundary because the person receiving the message reacts to the atmosphere of anger and misses the boundary. If you stay with the anger until it gives you its message and then moves through your system, you are calm and able to set the boundary clearly and firmly. Good boundary setting phrases are: "This isn't good for me" or "I am ending this conversation now" or "I am leaving and I will be back. . ." Always say when you will be back or it leaves the other person thinking you are avoiding conflict. When you are calm again is the time to talk about the anger.

There are times when boundaries aren't respected and you become endangered either physically or by the toxic environment. Anger can get you out of that situation. If someone in the environment is being violent and unstoppable, leave. Use your anger and fear, your outrage at what is happening, to get yourself to safety.

Relating from unconditional love does not require that you put up with anything others do or say. If your shared environment is limited by their actions, you will need to bring the issue to conflict resolution. If, over time, there is no cooperation in the matter, the relating begins to devolve. Finally, parting happens.

Partings can happen in the form of a time-out, distance from the situation, or they can be more permanent, a go-away parting.

Because anger is so toxic and sets off so much reactivation it is best to say something like, "I am feeling angry. I am having a reaction. I do not want to take it out on you or muddy the environment so I need some time to be with it and figure this out. I'll get back to you and let you know what I know, later." This leaves you centered and responsible, able to respond to your own reactions without blaming others.

SYSTEMS THINKING

Systems thinking begins with the understanding that everything is in flux. Learning to look at the world in this way and selecting your language to describe the world in this way will strengthen boundary setting and interrupt the reification.

This way of thinking allows us to think with the world instead of about the world. It will move us out of our rigid knowing and allow us to be able to be with the world as it is, unfolding.

Without the ability to think in process, we get into a lot of conflict within ourselves and with each other. We are led by our thinking process to believe that our opinions and points of view, and our reactions, are real. We become tragically trapped and closed. A closed system is a dead one. A static world is boring.

The skill to view the world and its people as fluid is the skill to think in process terms. The language of the 60's was process-oriented. "Hey what's happening, man?" A current example is "How's it going?"

Learning the language of mindfulness is a good way to get started. It is descriptive without story. Interpretations and opinions are stated as process.

COMMUNICATION BOUNDARIES

If you have studied about communication you have heard the term "I messages." Using "I messages" is an art. When I first learned about them I had a very strict teacher who would not let us use the word *you* at all. Everything had to be stated in neutral terms. For example:

I hate it when you leave the lid off the toothpaste.
BECOMES: *I hate it when I find the lid off the toothpaste.*

When you are angry I am afraid.
BECOMES: *I am afraid of anger,* or
When there is anger in the air I get distressed, or
I cannot hear what is being said when there is yelling.

Learning the art of "I messages" does several things. It makes your communication more neutral and less accusing, so you have a better chance of being heard. It allows the other to be less defensive. It stops you from taking responsibility for their reaction to what you say or from withholding because you are afraid of their reaction. If they react defensively, you merely restate your "I message."

believe

The greatest gift

I can conceive of having

From anyone

Is

To be seen by them

Heard by them

To be understood

And

Touched by them.

The greatest gift

I can give

Is

To see, hear, understand

And to touch

Another person.

When this is done

I feel

Contact has been made.

-Virginia Satir

Conflict Resolution

Conflict resolution from the brain that doesn't resolve a thing is
something we are all familiar with. It goes like this: I get an idea
in my head and hold it there and you get an idea in your head, too.
We both try to shove our ideas into each other's heads. We try to
force life to go our way and then wonder why we are weary and
unfulfilled. We want to be related on our terms. We want to be right.

The brain is in a hurry and uncomfortable with just being. It is
concerned with I, with me and mine. The brain is pessimistic,
negative, and likes lots of stimulation. It is emotionally immature
and much too busy to have any fun or be lighthearted. Guess what is
running the show when it comes to conflict?

We say we want intimacy, to be related, and then we act to the
contrary. We say we want someone to love, but what we really want
is someone to change or critically attack. We want someone to
unload on.

Conflict resolution from the heart takes time, patience, and
acceptance. It takes an expansive state. It takes maturity and the
ability to let the gross emotions pass so we can feel the subtle,
guiding emotions. It takes the ability to be where you are and notice
what there is to notice. It takes the willingness to accept your dissatisfaction and complaints as your friend. Your dissatisfaction and
complaints are telling you about your inner work. They are telling
you where you are contracted or they may be giving you a message
about the environment.

If you are leading an unexamined life and are not in tune with your
heart, your patterns will get acted out in relating. We need to
muster the will to work on ourselves and stop blaming others for our
unhappiness, despair, and pain. We need to get sufficiently aware of
what is going on inside ourselves.

We get stirred up in the presence of another. We find the vibrations that sway us off center. Conflict will show you where you need to grow. It will become the material for self-development. We all get hurt, angry, agitated, irritable, short-tempered. We all are vulnerable to being swayed by emotion and then we say and do all sorts of things. We have to reprogram our immature acting-out. Most emotion is irrational, but so is most thought. It does not make good sense to run your life by either of these. The developed observer that practices mindfulness will allow for a more mature relating with conflict.

We can develop the capacity to remain unaffected by the negative vibrations of others. When you can be in your personal space while also sharing that space with another, you have the room for conflict and its resolution.

You cannot avoid conflict. If you plan on being related, conflict will emerge. Find a way to be with conflict that is not damaging. Find a way that enhances your own growth and the growth of the other.

You have to be willing to give up the right to take out your disappointments and upsets on another person. You have to be willing to take care of the environment in which you have to relate. This means that you do not use it as a dumping ground. A really bad habit that many people have is to get home and to use the first part of reuniting with their families as a chance to complain about their day. This muddies the environment right away. You must remember that memory is always distorted and all reality is fundamentally subjective.

You have to be willing to stay in your autonomy, with yourself and to keep this clearly delineated from the other. You have to be aware of your tendency to have the other as an object. And you need to be breathing into the heart. Come into the heart. Feel the flow and the beating of the heart. Stay there as you meet with another. Relating is primary and objects are secondary.

In a complex and dynamic system, the tension between crises and transformation is central to the formation of the system. It is how we grow. There is an emergent quality, a symbiosis where the system is more than the sum of its parts. This is what will solve the dissonance. This is the magic that will transform. This is the power that will change you, change the other, and resolve the conflict!

Being related comes with great peace and with great pain. We have to be willing to accept both. Life is not just about happiness. We have to feel both the positive and the negative sides of life. We must learn to be honest and not back away from how we feel.

Feel what you feel, not what someone wants you to feel. Ask for what you want even though you may not get it. Take risks and do not always take the secure option. Say what is true for you in the moment even though it may change in the next moment.

A simple humor can develop when we have accepted that life includes darkness. Intimacy implies a certain anxiety. People who find themselves attached and stuck in the middle of battle will often erupt in laughter in the midst of it all. This is a moment of grace. This is a moment of expansion when we are lifted out of being stuck and are reminded that life is not designed to go our way. We can make friends with suffering.

A sense of humor and a dash of humility will go a long way in conflict resolution.

Something wonderful happens when we stop trying to get along and we stop trying to resolve things. Something wonderful happens when we can simply accept and be with dissonance. A subtle, unpredictable, and magical energy suddenly arrives and we are no longer separate or in conflict. We can wait for the ebb and flow of energies. When it is dissonant, we can stop thinking about it negatively. We can go into resonance with the difficulty. We give our attention until it dissolves. We get still, quiet, we feel and watch, and, like a cloud, it will disappear. This is much different than ignoring conflict. It is being mindful with conflict. It is joining with the trouble and including it.

Stop trying and simply state what is going on with you, on your side of the boundary. Wait and it will resolve. Hold your experience, however negative, and describe it within the observer state. Have curiosity and interest in it. Be compassionate with it, allowing it to express and open to what you need to see about it. Suspend pretense and judgment. See if you can eliminate analyzing, criticizing, or changing it.

Silence is the language of God. Plato said, "Two things alone cannot be satisfactorily united without a third; for there must be some bond between them drawing them together." Let the alchemy of spirit resolve what is troubling you or what is different between you. You must state what is happening on your side of the boundary. You must listen to what is happening on their side of the boundary. By feeling directly and saying what is happening, it gets it out of the insane recycling of the brain and gives it to something bigger.

Speak about frustration, speak about disappointment, speak from your heart; conflict is a gift. After the speaking, you must wait. In the silence, there will be a stirring on your behalf.

It works like synchronization. If you place a number of pendulum clocks in a room together, at first they all tick to a different beat, but if you leave them for a time and come back, they will all be ticking together. They will be synchronized. This is how the background works. It connects us eventually and we will again tick together. Learn to trust this background.

I have developed, used, and tested the following model for conflict resolution. It is designed to dramatically slow down communication. It provides a structural dialogue. This allows for body consciousness and for each person to be aware of themselves as the communication is happening. It helps people distinguish between their own issues and the issues of others. The structure helps us keep our needed boundaries and helps prevent us from violating the boundaries of others.

The process is set up like a game. It uses the boundaries of the

Touch and Go model. Many people who have used the game in their personal relating, at work, in their families, and who have mastered it report that it keeps them aware and helps develop the needed skills of healthy relating. The process makes them deal with the issue that allows them to grow. It keeps the relating clean, gives feelings a voice. It provides an environment to talk without blame.

This process eliminates a lot of analyzing and comments or criticism. It simply gives the opportunity for each person to be listened to and to be responsible for being heard. It gives each person an opportunity to listen to another. Listening does not mean agreement; it simply is giving your attention to another and hearing how life is for them at the time of the listening. It is not set up to discuss things and it is not set up to resolve things. Remember, it is never technique that makes anything happen. This process simply establishes the structure that allows the observer to do the observing, that allows each person to do their own self-examination, and that maintains the boundaries needed for each person to remain autonomous.

A Formula for Learning Conflict Resolution

This formula slows the communication process down enough for learning.

You will need:

1. Two pads of paper for each person, each pad a different color.

2. A specific time to meet once a week for an hour, or no more than one & 1/2 hours (extend only if things are going well).

Ground rules:

1. Do with another person; also can be adapted to be used with a group or you can do it by yourself.

2. If one of the people is emotionally upset at the time of the scheduled meeting, set a definite new time and keep that time no matter what.

3. During the week, give up the right to voice any complaints. This means complaints about work and other people, too.

4. Save all complaints for the scheduled meeting.

① Step one:

1. Each person keeps track of their complaints on a pad of paper.

2. Write each complaint on a separate sheet of paper in the pad.

3. When writing complaints it is best to use immediate, direct language. Clear and to the point, not a lot of explanation or logic (it dilutes your message).

4. Stay on your own side by using statements about yourself.

5. Avoid blaming words. Avoid using the word *you*.

EXAMPLES:

> I'm afraid of yelling and shouting.
>
> I don't like the lid off the toothpaste.
>
> I'm concerned about our eating habits.

REMEMBER: do not blame the other for your feelings (don't use the word *you*), simply state how you are feeling and the circumstances that were or are present when you were or are feeling those feelings.

Before the meeting you may want to rewrite your complaints so they reflect what you are feeling in your heart, rather than a reaction. Sit quietly by yourself, breathe into your heart and ask it how it feels.

2 STEP TWO:

1. Bring complaints to the meeting.

2. Use a table between you. Divide it in half.

3. Take a moment to hold hands, close your eyes, and breathe into the heart. Open your eyes and gaze at each other, staying with your own heart until you are ready to begin. Hold each other in your attention, focused, caring, without pretense, without judgment, without criticism. Be honest and kind, have fun.

3 STEP THREE:

1. Person "a" puts their complaints on their side of the table, simply stating them without an attitude.

2. Person "b" sets aside any reaction or disagreement and simply listens to "a".

3. "b" makes no comment other than "Thank you" or "Could you say more about that, I don't quite get what you are saying."

4. "b" has the job of making sure "a" is heard completely. Being heard does not mean "b" agrees with what is being put on the table, but simply that "b" has heard it.

5. "b" can jot any "charged" reactions down on a separate, different color pad than they used during the week, again using a separate sheet for each reaction.

Important: do the writing only after "a" has been completely heard, not while they are still talking. Again, show no attitude or reaction; simply write out your response. If you let your reactions spill out into the environment, it limits the safety for communication. Yes, this does take some maturity!

④ STEP FOUR:

Then it switches.

1. "a" listens while "b" puts their complaints on the table.

2. "a" has the job of making sure "b" is heard completely.

3. If "a" has a strong, "charged" reaction to something, they record it on a separate colored pad; different than the color they used all week.

⑤ STEP FIVE:

1. After each has had a turn to put out all the complaints for the week, they do another round.

2. "b" goes first and puts down all of their reactions or "charged" items (which they recorded after listening to "a" on their second color of paper) and "a" listens.

3. "a" puts out all of their reactions (the ones they wrote after listening to "b", on their second color paper), "b" listens.

⑥ STEP SIX:

Now comes the difficult part:

1. Each person looks at their own side of the table, at the complaints and reactions they have set out on the table.

2. Each person picks back up any complaints or reactions that now have a high emotional charge, as they read them, from their own side of the table. Give no advice to one another over this.

3. They pick them up because they are not ready for discussion or resolution while they are still *charged*. More inner work is required.

This allows both people to know what issues the other is working on in their own inner work.

4. Later the other will bring the charged issues back to the table after they have done their own self-examination. When the issues are no longer charged, at a later time they can be shared, letting the partner know what process and discovery was made during their inner work.

7 STEP SEVEN:

What is left on the table is sorted:

1. Non-issues, no problem, no resolution needed (often just having the other listen is enough to clear it up).

2. Issues on which we agree to disagree, no emotional charge. We are different.

3. Issues for discussion, each person owning their own part, committed to coming up with a resolution that will work for both people.

4. There may be some request to make of each other.

> When you make a request it is important to allow that the response may be no, or they may want to make a counteroffer.

> If there is no room for "no," then it is a demand.

> Demands are disrespectful and don't get good results.

5. Select a new color pad for the next week.

6. Take a moment to give thanks for the process and for the guidance and wisdom that develops. Give thanks for willingness to be vulnerable and participate. Thank the other person and adjourn the meeting.

7. Again give up the right to complain during the following week.

Love, Commitment, Marriage

What we call falling in love is an insufficient basis for ongoing relating. It simply is not enough. Relating based on the pursuit of romance will eventually lead to resentment, demands, unfulfilled expectations, and upset.

Your only chance to be truly alive is to find out how to meet your own essential nature and live from there. That is when we are fulfilled. That is when we are most beautiful and attractive. We are not precious because someone else thinks so. We are precious just because.

The development of relating takes time. It takes unfolding. We cannot hurry the process. When we are in a hurry, we do not let something be shown to us. We do not know how to experience someone so we would rather have them explain who they are. We have to be around someone long enough and in a variety of different circumstances to really know if they are authentic.

We cannot tell if someone is authentic by what they say. Ignore what they say and look at who they are being over time. There is a big difference between what someone says as a description of who they are and what they want and who they are without words.

We have to pass the stage of desire for a certain kind of relating. We have to pass the stage of insight before we try to talk about our understanding of relating. An understanding about relating is not relating. A desire for a certain kind of relating does not mean we have the consciousness to have that kind of relating.

Insight and understanding need to translate into action and show in our life. Truth becomes demonstrated in our living. It flows out onto others without our speaking, without our effort, and attracts others who can vibrate with our vibration. Stop relating by talking about relating.

Move from a concern with relationship, closeness, stability, and familiarity to a concern with process, connection, and creation.

If you sexualize the relating too soon, the pursuit of pleasure takes over and you miss important information being shown to you about the other. Delay, wait, let the friendship evolve. Let the foundation be built. Let spirit tell you when it is time for the physical. Sexually expressing intimacy is sacred. Do not diminish this with lust and passion, by being in a hurry.

We cannot give up our own integrity on behalf of another and still retain it. If another person is not willing to wait, perhaps they are not the right person.

It is best to suspect and resist love at first sight. Moments of intimacy itself are not enough to sustain long-term relating such as marriage. If we can stay ourselves over time with another, then we may consider marriage. Respect, cooperation, and dialogue are the best ingredients for marriage. Marriage gives structure. Marriage can give a strong container for growth and ease and safety and self expression. Without a container, you have content without sufficient context and relating can remain on the surface.

Commitment evolves. We find ourselves committed. It is not an action. Commitment as an action or idea falls short of the true state of commitment. If you have a long-term commitment and are unhappy, perhaps you have become too close and need to build some distance into your relating. Distance does wonders for commitment. So does just hanging out with someone in silence and letting your energies mingle and heal. Remember the clocks that hang out in the background and then begin ticking together? It is the same with people.

It is good to get away together as a couple in a new setting. It lets you see what may be off in the environment of your home. Yearly evaluation of your commitment, your agreements, and your gratitude to each other and to spirit is a good way to maintain the health of your joining.

If you are trying to change something about your relating, it helps to stop and include and accept whatever is happening. The more you try to change something, the worse it gets. When we try to change another person, they will continue to do the things we do not like until we accept them as they are. True love is unconditional.

It is not true that it takes two people to change a relationship. We cannot change another. We can only be willing to have ourself be changed. We get changed by Grace and notice it through awareness. As we are changed and hold the change long enough, not giving into the pull back into old patterns, the whole system will change. Everything around us will change without our effort! Other people will change and the change sometimes means they will leave. We may refuse to change because we are afraid they will leave. Remember that Spirit is in charge of change.

And now let us turn to love. Love is not an action. Love is not a thing. Love is a condition. Love is everywhere, moving through everything. Love is accepting and kind and generous and patient. Love is that into which we were born and that which has never, ever left us. We may have become contracted and unable to register love but that is not the fault of love. Come back home to love. We need not search for it any further than our heart. We are loved. That love is inclusive, everyone is included whether they believe it or not. We have always been loved. We will always be loved. We can do nothing to send love away. Come home to love. It is the place of belonging.

Sacred Sexuality

We are not entitled to good sex, frequent sex, or any sex. It is not an inherent human right. Yet in so many relationships, this is what people are complaining about. This is what so many people are demanding.

The nature of sex is distorted when people become property, and expectations and desires become rights. We have turned sex into pursuit and evidence that we are cared for. We are focused on technique, release, gratification, and the pursuit of pleasure for the sake of pleasure. We are focused on the symbols of romance. Many are surprised to hear or learn that anything else is possible.

Good sex, good technique, is not experience of sexual union. Genital sensation and manipulation fall way short of what is possible. In fact, when we focus on the genitals and not the whole body, including the emotions and the heart, the experience is not enhancing or nourishing. We get a sharp genital pleasure and a release, depleting the nervous energetic system and we are let down, disappointed, unfulfilled, and sleepy. Then we think that more will be better.

When we genitalize sex and depersonalize sex, the experience does not penetrate the body, mind, and heart. It shoots energy out of the system and leaves us tired and scattered. It is a lonely act.

It may be fun, but screwing does nothing to enhance or energize relating. Making love, however, does! The whole body is sexual. The body can orgasm from the heart. The body can orgasm from its pulse points. When you merge with another in intimacy, the experience includes the whole body. You cannot make this happen. It happens to you when you are safe and can take the time. We are in such a hurry. We need to slow down and stop pursuing. We need to stop trying so hard. The electromagnetic output of the heart is 5,000 times more that the electromagnetic output of the brain. Let the heart lead.

The difference in expressing love and having sex is detected in how you feel afterward. In expressing love, the afterward goes on and on and then gently dissipates. After lovemaking, we see the other and ourself a little differently. We have been changed by the event. Intimacy has done its work with us. We have been taken into a higher state. There is a gentle gladness and gratitude.

True sexuality in a sacred context can be intimidating—the same intimidation that accompanies intimacy. Remaining conscious for sex is challenging. We need to learn to get still and quiet inside, ready to receive the gift.

It is easier to remain in dissociated patterns of sexual behavior, in ideas of what to do. We move into stylized modes of having sex to avoid the tension of not knowing what to do. When we sexualize the relating too soon, we jump over the unfolding necessary to be conscious. We miss being led by the unfolding. We have sex as a good idea, a willful act. When we are attempting to make something happen, we are unable to be in touch with timing.

Timing is everything. If we get ahead of the life force or lag behind, we will not be found and carried. If we get carried into intimacy and have no place to return, we can remain disoriented and ungrounded. If we are not safe with the other person, we may find that their energy is not good for us. We may lose ourselves in them, lost in fusion.

Having sex with someone who is angry or sad co-mingles those energies and can damage. Fantasy is dissociated sex, sex in the head, not in present time. When someone is in fantasy, they are not available for intimacy. Fantasy takes place in thinking. Fantasy is for those who are unable or unwilling to be present, to experience intimacy. Pornography is dissociation, where fantasy is more important than the present. Images may happen during sex but they are dreamlike and not associated with people or body parts. Sex from need is goal oriented and therefore dead.

Before being sexual with someone, we need to make sure that each of us is free from discord, that we are not in the middle of conflict. Taking sex away from the sacred and letting our negative emotions be expressed sexually is a desecration of this sacred meeting.

The mischief around sex is because of the fear of intimacy. We are afraid of intimacy with God and therefore with each other. There really is no such thing as sexual energy. There is energy, expressed sexually. Find out what your purpose is before venturing into the sexual realm.

Do you have sex to get to glory and the uplifted state or are you experiencing glory and expressing it sexually? These are two widely separated experiences!

Sex when we are connected is spontaneous, curious, and playful. Orgasm is the gift, arising out of feelings felt moment to moment, not the goal. The language of sex is softness without words. It is flowing and inclusive, tolerant and accepting. The language of sex is patient. We can learn to wait to be shown what to do by the life force, by the unfolding of a sacred event. This kind of sexual meeting nourishes your bodies, your psyches, your container rather than dissipating them and leaving you depleted.

When couples are having trouble sexually or relationally—these two often go together—I will often have them negotiate a sexual vacation for a while. The result of these sexual vacations is an increase in intimacy.

It is unpopular, I know, to have to wait for sex. Invitation, ceremony, taking time, the consent of Spirit is foreign to our way of thinking. Remember that romance is a brain thing and infatuation is empty and makes us love-blind. Great sex takes three! It includes taking in Spirit, it includes acknowledging the sacred background in which you participate.

One of the great barriers to sex is a tense mind. Relaxing the mind is a slow process. We will not let the mind relax if we are not safe. We can only be safe when we can be resting in a larger presence, allowing it to lead us. We need a safe place where we can be centered enough to allow for the discomfort of being stirred, able to fully be in our bodies and really feeling all there is to feel, with technique set aside, vulnerable, with patience and acceptance and a willingness to be taught.

"Life

is a Spiritual journey

to know truth,

to find the true Self.

Anything else is disappointing."

-JB

PART FOUR

The Journey

The Journey

Given what is available in the heights of glorious intimacy, why do we settle for far less?

We can see that our training does not lead us directly toward the expanded state of being. Our intuition holds out, though, and eventually we will all get disillusioned with the ordinary and reach out for the extraordinary. We will eventually reach for the expanded heights.

In the background, behind all of our training and history in this place in consciousness where we are connected, there is no effort or searching, no loneliness, no aggressive willfulness, only peace and faith and rest.

We find that we are already related. We all belong to the background, the life force, that hold us, runs through all, is connecting all. It is where we come from and where we will return.

Look into the background and welcome the Creator into your heart, into your world, into your cells. Vibrate together for without the eternal, life is thin and dry.

In the heart, there is a submerged center. It is the wisdom center of your own heart's Self, your heart of hearts, your own essential nature. This wisdom center is your personal, secret place constituted of the most high. It is a center of divine wisdom.

The secret key to this center is awareness. The secret key to awareness is the breath. Focus your attention on your breath inside and wait.

This total stillness is where your yearning will be fulfilled. The Holy Divine river flows through all and is in all and available to all through expanded consciousness.

When you are in the contracted state, you have merely forgotten. When you are contracted, it does not mean that you are not sacred or that the divine has forgotten you.

Trust in a force beyond what you can see. Turn your will and your life over to that life force. Invite the unfolding of the sacred pattern trapped in the heart. See the world and each other through God's heart.

The Creator creates creation. We are of the creation. We are creation, individualized. All creation rises out of creation and dissolves back into the Creator. Be silent and be held and safe at last.

All is leading home. We are all going home to the heart of the essential Self. We don't even have to wait to experience it. We can experience it now.

Illumination is the ability to see, to know without knowing. To see the light of the essential heart-Self with our extended vision, our spiritual sight. It is a joyous experience, an experience of ecstasy. We can see the light and the holiness in all and through all. All of the instruction to the intellect is useless. The experience is led by the heart and followed by the intellect.

As outer activity decreases, the inner world opens. Life becomes deeper and richer, fulfilling.

We need to take an independent look and trust our insides, trust our intuitive knowing. We are essentially good and in the uplifted state our goodness is expressed into the world. There is only one mind. There is only one essential Self. There is only one Source. Anything you want to know can be sensed directly by getting still and going into the wisdom place inside. Like all that is difficult, it takes practice. Practice going inside.

There is nothing wrong. All is unfolding in a divine way, with order. It is all a mystery we can learn to welcome. Each of us is designed to unfold. All of life is designed to help us become whole. Even the distractions, the troubles help our unfolding.

The path to wholeness is sacred. The benefit of the path is expansion, understanding beyond words. Joy, wonderment, love, and compassion become your intimate friends.

Hold your life in prayerful stillness until consciousness rids you of any pretense. Give up self-glorification and invite the creation to use you.

Bloom into all you can be. Peace begins inside with each of us. Faith is a state of consciousness, reached through devotion, through turning inside. There is no outer battle more important than the one inside ourselves. Do we choose the world or do we choose the highest?

The highest is what will give ecstasy, intimacy, peace, and rest. The fruit of the spiritual life is rest. When you are at rest, what rises up inside your heart is gratitude. We know gratitude for the precious gift of a life. Gratitude rises up for the teachers along the way, gratitude for the help, for the guidance, for the wisdom that leaks through the illusion.

We feel gratitude for the yearning to be expanded and purified, for this, too, is a gift. We have gratitude for the body that registers higher consciousness. We give gratitude for the heart that sweeps us out of our ideas.

We have gratitude for Grace—sweet, precious, delicious Grace— kissing our lives so sweetly. Grace lifts us out of misery and works in us and through us out into the world.

We relax as we make our home in the eternal heart and know that all is well.

The End....The Beginning

Book List

A Parenthesis in Eternity, Joel S. Goldsmith

A Return to Love, Marianne Williamson

A Woman's Worth, Marianne Williamson

At the Leading Edge: New Visions of Science, Spirituality, and Society, edited by Michael Toms

Beyond Codependence and Getting Better All the Time, Melody Beattie

Challenge of the Heart: Love, Sex, and Intimacy in Changing Times, edited by John Welwood

Codependent No More: How to Stop Controlling Others and Start Caring for Yourself, Melody Beattie

Conscious Loving: A Way to Be Fully Together Without Giving up Yourself, Gay Hendricks, Kathlyn Hendricks

Do I Have to Give Up Me to Be Loved By You? Jordan Paul, Margaret Paul

Divorce Busting, Michele Weiner-Davis

Escape from Intimacy: Untangling the "Love" Addiction: Sex, Romance, Relationships, Anne Wilson Schaef

Facing Love Addiction: Giving Yourself the Power to Change the Way You Love, Pia Mellody

From Conflict to Caring: An In-depth Program for Creating Loving Relationships, Jordan Paul, Margaret Paul

Full Catastrophe Living, Jon Kabat-Zinn

Getting the Love You Want, Harville Hendrix

Guilt is the Teacher; Love is the Lesson, Joan Borysenko

Handbook to Higher Consciousness, Ken Keyes

I and Thou, Martin Buber

If the Buddha Dated, Charlotte Kasl

Intimate Partners, Patterns in Love and Marriage, Maggie Scarf

Intimate Relationships: Why They Do and Do Not Work,
Stephen Wolinsky

Journey of Awakening: A Meditator's Guidebook, Ram Dass

*Meeting the Shadow: The Hidden Power of the Dark Side of Human
Nature,* edited by Connie Zweig and Jeremiah Abrams

Mysticism and the New Physics, Michael Talbot

Obsessive Love: When it Hurts Too Much to Let Go, Susan Forward

Ordinary People as Monks and Mystics: Lifestyles for Self-discovery,
Marsha Sinetar

No Boundary: Eastern and Western Approaches to Personal Growth,
Ken Wilbur

Parenting With Love and Logic: Teaching Children Responsibility,
Foster Cline, Jim Fay

Play of Consciousness, Swami Muktananda

Practical Mysticism, Evelyn Underhill

Seat of the Soul, Gary Zukav

Spiritual Emergency, edited by Stanislov Grof and Christina Grof

Stalking the Wild Pendulum: On the Mechanics of Consciousness,
Itzhak Bentov

Start Where You Are: A Guide to Compassionate Living, Pema Chodron

Taking the Quantum Leap: The New Physics to Nonscientists,
Fred Wolf

That Which Transpires Behind That Which Appears:
The Experience of Sufism, Pir Vilayat Inayat Khan

The Art of Loving, Erich Fromm

The Atman Project, Ken Wilbur

The Courage to Be Yourself: A Woman's Guide to Growing Beyond
Emotional Dependence, Sue Patton Thoele

The Dance of Anger, Harriet Lerner

The Dance of Connection, Harriet Lerner

The Dance of Intimacy, Harriet Lerner

The Dark Side of the Light Chasers: Reclaiming Your Power, Creativity,
Brilliance, and Dreams, Debbie Ford

The Enfolding-Unfolding Universe: A Conversation with David Bohm.

The Heart's Code: Tapping the Wisdom and Power of Our Heart Energy,
Paul Pearsal

The Heart of The Soul; Emotional Awareness, Gary Zukav, Linda Francis

The Holographic Universe, Michael Talbot

The Holotropic Mind: The Three Levels of Human Consciousness and How
They Shape Our Lives, Stanislov Grof

The Intimate Enemy: How to Fight Fair in Love and Marriage,
George R. Back and Peter Wyden

The Legacy of the Heart: The Spiritual Advantages of a Painful Childhood,
Wayne Muller

*The Lost Art of Listening: How Learning to Listen Can Improve
Relationships*, Michael P. Nichols

The New Peoplemaking, Virginia Satir

The Only Dance There Is, Ram Dass

The Path to Love: Renewing the Power of Spirit in Your Life,
Deepak Chopra

The Power of Now, Ekhart Tolle

The Road Less Traveled, F. Scott Peck

The Tibetan Book of Living and Dying, Sogyal Rinpoche

The Upanishads: Breath of the Eternal, translated by Swami
Prabhavananda and Frederick Manchester

The Web of Life, Fritjof Capra

12 Steps to Self-Parenting, Philip Oliver-Diaz,
Patricia A. O'Gorman

*Wherever You Go There You Are: Mindfulness Meditation
in Everyday Life*, Jon Kabat-Zinn

When Society is an Addict, Anne Wilson Scheaf

Wholeness and the Implicate Order, David Bohm

Women, Sex, and Addiction, Charlottle Davis Kasl

An Invitation

This is an invitation for you to come to a retreat in New Mexico. The retreats begin at 2 p.m. on Friday and end at 5 p.m. on Sunday. You can find a retreat schedule at: www.Spiritrelationship.com. Call 505-266-1500 to have a schedule mailed to you. Leave your name and address. Fax: 505-384-2260.

If you would like Judy to have a workshop in your area or you would like her to speak at an event, please contact the above numbers or write to her at:

Judy Borich
P.O. Box 2185
Tijeras, New Mexico 87059

Would you like to be on our mailing list? Mailing lists are used only for sending out our information and are never rented, sold, or given to anyone else. Please contact Judy Borich at JBorich@aol.com if you would like to be on our mailing list and receive information on upcoming retreats and other events.

Order Form

Fax orders: 505-384-2260

Telephone orders: Call 505-266-1500. You may use Visa or MasterCard. Leave name on card, address for card, card number, and expiration date.

On-line orders: www.Spiritrelationship.com.

Postal orders: Interact Publishing, Judy Borich
                 P.O. Box 2185 • Tijeras, NM 87059 • USA

Please send_____copies of *Touch and Go the Nature of Intimacy, Relating in the Coming Times*. I understand that I may return any books for a full refund for any reason.

Company name: _____

Name: _____

Address: _____

City: _____ State: _____ Zip: _____

Telephone (   ) _____

Please send $15.95. Shipping and Handling is $6.50 for the first book and $4.00 for each additional book.

Payment: ❑ Check   ❑ Credit Card: ❑ VISA   ❑ MasterCard

Card number: _____

Billing Address on card (if different than above): _____

_____

Exp. date: _____

E-mail: _____

"There is a vitality,

a life force, an energy, a quickening

that is translated through you into action;

and because there is only one of you in

all time, this expression is unique.

If you block it, it will never exist

through any other medium and it will be lost.

The world will not have it.

You must keep that channel open.

It is not for you to determine how good it is,

nor how valuable.

Nor how it compares with other expressions.

It is for you to keep it yours,

clearly and directly."

- Martha Graham